Geo. Dance   H.Adlard

JOSEPH HAYDN.

LIFE OF HAYDN

BY

LOUIS NOHL.

TRANSLATED FROM THE GERMAN

BY

GEORGE P. UPTON.

" Heart and soul must be free."

SEVENTH EDITION.

CHICAGO:

A. C. McCLURG & COMPANY.

1902.

Republished, 1970
Scholarly Press, 22929 Industrial Drive East
St. Clair Shores, Michigan 48080

Nohl, Ludwig, 1831-1885.
    Life of Haydn, by Louis Nohl. Translated from the German by George P. Upton. St. Clair Shores, Mich., Scholarly Press, 1970.

    195 p. port. 21 cm.

    Reprint of the 1902 ed.

    1. Haydn, Joseph, 1732-1809.

ML410.H4N8 1970   ' 780'.924 [B]   · 75-115259
ISBN 0-403-00343-1   MARC
    Library of Congress   70 [4]   MN

INTRODUCTION

THE abridged Life of Haydn, by Dr. Nohl, prepared originally as a contribution to a series of
biographies, which is issued in popular form in
Germany, is so simple in its narrative, that it would
hardly need an introduction, were its subject-mat-
ter confined to the record of Haydn's life, with its
many musical triumphs, or to the portraiture of
this genial, child-like and lovable master. The
trials and troubles of his youth, their intensification
in his married life, his marvelous musical progress,
his seclusion at Eisenstadt, his visits to London
and his introduction to its gay world in his old age,
followed by such wonderful musical triumphs, make
a story of extraordinary personal interest, which
the author has heightened with numerous anecdotes,
illustrating his rare sweetness and geniality. There
are many discursions, however, in the work, in
which Dr. Nohl analyzes the component parts of
Haydn's musical creations, and traces the effect of
his predecessors as well as of his cotemporaries upon
his development as an artist. To understand these,
it must be remembered that the author deals with
music from a philosophical standpoint, choosing

Schopenhauer for his authority, the philosopher whom Wagner admires so much, and who makes the Will the basis of all phenomena. Applied in a musical sense therefore, music is not a matter of sweet sounds, whether melody or harmony, nor is its principal office the creation of pleasure by these sounds, but it is the chief agent of the Will in giving expression to its impulses. What this theory is, has been stated by Richard Wagner himself in his "Essay on Beethoven," in the following words: "The mere element of music, as an idea of the world, is not beheld by us, but felt instead, in the depths of consciousness, and we understand that idea to be an immediate revelation of the unity of the Will, which, proceeding from the unity of human nature, incontrovertibly exhibits itself to our consciousness, as unity with universal nature also, which indeed we likewise perceive through sound." The definition will afford a clue to some of the author's statements, and may help to make clearer some of his musical analyses. The rest of the work may safely be left to the reader. It is the record of the life not only of a great musician, but of a lovable man, who is known to this day among his own people, though almost a century has elapsed since his death, by the endearing appellation of "Papa."

G. P. U.

CONTENTS.

CHAPTER I.

HIS YOUTH AND EARLY STUDIES.

CHAPTER II.

AT PRINCE ESTERHAZY'S.

CHAPTER III.

THE FIRST LONDON JOURNEY.

CHAPTER IV.

THE EMPEROR'S HYMN—THE CREATION AND THE SEASONS.

THE LIFE OF HAYDN.

CHAPTER I.

1732—1753.

HIS YOUTH AND EARLY STUDIES.

Haydn's Birth and Family—His Early Talent—First Studies with Frankh—Chapel-boy at St. Stephen's—Reutter's Instructions—Early Compositions—His Mischievous Tricks and Dismissal—Anecdote of Maria Theresa—Acquaintance with Metastasio—Influence of Philip Emanuel Bach—The Origin of his First Opera, "The Devil on Two Sticks."

"SEE, my dear Hummel, the house in which Haydn was born; to think that so great a man should have first seen the light in a peasant's wretched cottage." Such were the words of Beethoven, upon his death-bed in 1827, as he spoke of the father of the symphony and quartet, both of which he himself brought to their highest perfection.

Joseph Haydn was born March 31, 1732, at the market-town of Rohrau, near Bruck, on the river Leitha, which at that point separates

Lower Austria from Hungary. The little place belonged to the Counts Harrach, who erected a memorial to his honor in their park upon his return from his London triumphs in 1795.

Haydn's father was a wheelwright, and the craft had long been followed by the family. He had traveled as a master-workman, and in his wanderings had been, it is said, as far as Frankfort-on-Main. His marriage was blessed with twelve children, six of whom died very young. They were brought up religiously in the Catholic faith, and as they were poor, they were also accustomed to economy and industry. In his old age, Haydn said: "My parents were so strict in their lessons of neatness and order, even in my earliest youth, that at last these habits became a second nature." His mother watched over him most tenderly, but his father alone lived to enjoy the recompense of such care, when his son was installed as Capellmeister. The manner in which he remembered his mother's grave many years later in his will reveals the strength of her influence.

His father, who was "by nature a great lover of music," had a fair tenor voice, and during

his travels accompanied himself on the harp
without knowing a note. After the day's toil,
the family sang together, and even when an
old man, Haydn recalled with much emotion
these musical pleasures of his boyhood. The
little "Sepperl," as he was called, astonished
them all with the correctness of his ear and
the sweetness of his voice, and always sang
his short simple pieces to his father in a correct manner. More than this, he closely imitated the handling of a violin-bow with a little stick, and upon one such occasion a relative,
from the neighborhood, observed the remarkable feeling for strict tone and time, in the five-
year-old boy. This relative, who was the
schoolmaster and choir-leader in the neighboring town of Hainburg, took the lad, who
was intended for the priesthood, to that place,
that he might study the art which it was
thought would undoubtedly open a way to the
accomplishment of this purpose. After this,
Haydn only returned home as a visitor, but
that he remembered it and his poor relatives
all his life with esteem and affection, is evi-
denced by this remark in his old age: "I live
not so much for myself as for my poor rela-

tives to whom I would leave something after my death." His " Biographical Notices " say he was so little ashamed of his humble origin that he often spoke of it himself. In his will, he remembers the parish priest and school-teacher as well as the poor children of his humble birth-place. In 1795, when he revisited it, upon the occasion of the dedication of the Harrach memorial, before alluded to, he knelt down in the familiar old sitting-room, kissed its threshold, and pointed out the settle where he had once displayed in sport that childish musical skill which was the indication of his subsequent grand artistic career. " The young may learn from my example that something may come out of nothing; what I am is entirely the result of the most pressing necessity," he once said, as he recalled his humble antecedents.

In Hainburg, Haydn learned the musical rudiments and studied other branches necessary to youth, with his cousin Matthias Frankh. In an autobiographical sketch, about the year 1776, which may be found in the " *Musiker-briefe*" (Leipsic, 1873, second edition), he says: " Almighty God, to whom I give thanks

for all His unnumbered mercies, bestowed upon
me such musical facility that even in my sixth
year I sang with confidence several masses in
the church choir, and could play a little on the
piano and violin." Besides this, he learned
there the nature of all the ordinary instruments,
and could play upon most of them. "I thank
this man, even in his grave, for making me
work so hard, though I used to get more blows
than food," runs one of his later humorous con-
fessions. Unfortunately, the latter complaint
corresponded to the rest of his treatment in
his cousin's house. "I could not help observing, much to my distress, that I was getting
very dirty, and though I was quite vain of my
person, I could not always prevent the spots
upon my clothes from showing, of which I
was greatly ashamed—in fact, I was a little
urchin," he says at another time. Even at
that time he wore a wig, " for the sake of clean-
liness," without which it is almost impossible
to imagine "Papa Haydn."

Of the style of musical instruction in Hainburg, we have at least one example. It was
in Passion week, a time of numerous proces-
sions. Frankh was in great trouble, owing to

the death of his kettle-drummer, but espying little "Sepperl," he bethought himself that he could quickly learn. He showed him how to play and then left him. The lad took a basket, such as the peasants use for holding flour in their baking, covered it over with a cloth, placed it upon a finely upholstered chair, and drummed away with so much spirit that he did not observe the flour had sifted out and ruined the chair. He was reprimanded, as usual, but his teacher's wrath was appeased when he noticed how quickly Joseph had become a skillful drummer. As he was at that time very short in stature, he could not reach up to the man who had been accustomed to carry the drum, which necessitated the employment of a smaller man, and, as unfortunately he was a hunchback, it excited much laughter in the procession. But Haydn in this manner gained a thoroughly practical knowledge of the instrument and, as is well known, the drum-parts in his symphonies are of special importance. He was the first to give to this instrument a thorough individuality and a separate artistic purpose in instrumental music. He was very proud of his skill, and, as we shall see farther on, his ideas were of great assistance to a kettle-drummer in London.

This first practical result convinced his teacher that Haydn was destined for a musical career. His systematic industry was universally praised, and his agreeable voice was his best personal recommendation. The result was, that after two years of study he went to Vienna, under happy, we may even say the happiest, of auspices.

The Hainburg pastor was a warm friend of Hofcapellmeister Reutter. It happened that the latter, journeying from Vienna on business, passed through Hainburg and made the pastor a short visit. During his stay he mentioned the purpose of his journey, namely, the engagement of boys with sufficient talent as well as good voices for choir service. The pastor at once thought of Joseph. Reutter desired to see this clever lad. He made his appearance. Reutter said to him: "Can you trill, my little man?" Joseph, thinking perhaps that he ought not to know more than people above him, replied to the question: "My teacher even can not do that." "Look here," said Reutter, "I will trill for you. Pay attention and see

how I do it." He had scarcely finished, when
Haydn stood before him with the utmost confidence and after two attempts trilled so per-
fectly that Reutter in astonishment cried out,
" bravo," drew out of his pocket a seventeen-
kreuzer piece, and presented it to the little
virtuoso. This incident is related by Dies, the
painter, who was intimate with Haydn from
1805 until his death, and who published in
1810 the very interesting " Biographical Notices" of him.

The little fellow meanwhile devoted himself
to vocal practice until his eighth year, when he
was to enter the chapel, for the Hofcapellmeister had made this stipulation when he promised the father to advance his son. As he
could find no teacher who was versed in the
rules, he studied by himself, and following the
natural method, learned to sing the scales and
made such rapid progress that when he went
to Vienna, Reutter was astonished at his facility.

The chapel was that of St. Stephen. In
addition to frequent religious services, the boys
were also obliged to work at various kinds of
outside labor, so that their musical improve-
ment was considerably hindered. In spite of

this, Haydn says that besides his vocal practice, he studied the piano and violin with very
good masters, and received much praise for his
singing, both at church and court.   The general course of studies included only the scant-
iest instruction in religion, writing, ciphering
and Latin ; and art, the most important of all
to him, was so much worse off that at last he
became his own teacher again.   Reutter troubled himself very little about his chapel-schol-
ars, and was a very imperious master besides;
" and yet," said Haydn afterward, " I was not
a complete master of any instrument, but I knew
the quality and action of all.   I was no mean
pianist and singer, and could play violin concertos."   Singing chiefly occupied his time
and strength, for he contended that a German
instrumental composer must first master vocal
study in order to write melodies.   He considered this all his life as of the greatest importance and often complained because so few composers understood it.   Among all the results of
his youthful artistic training. secured in his
ten years' chapel service in Vienna, these two
were the most important.   He continually
heard *a capella*, that is, pure choral music

with its contrapuntal texture, and also learned all forms of solo singing and instrumental
music, and so thoroughly also that he was at
home in all of them.   And yet, "honest Reutter" had only given him two lessons in musical theory!

Dies relates other characteristic anecdotes
of his youthful time.   Notwithstanding his
advancement had been neglected, Joseph was
contented with his position, and for this reason only, that Reutter was so delighted with
his talent that he told his father if he had
twelve sons he would take care of all of them.
Two of his brothers indeed came to the chapel, one of them Michael Haydn, afterward
Capellmeister at Salzburg, with whom Mozart's biography has made us acquainted,
and Joseph had the "infinite pleasure" of
being compelled to instruct them.   Even
under such circumstances, he busily occupied himself with composition.   Every piece
of paper that came into his hands he covered
with staves, though with much trouble, and
stuck them full of notes, for he imagined it was
all right if he only had his paper full.   At one
time Reutter surprised him just at the moment

when he had stretched out before him a paper more than a yard long, with a *Salve Regina* for twelve voices, sketched upon it. "Ha! what are you doing, my little fellow?" said he. But when he saw the long paper he laughed heartily at the plentiful rows of *Salves*, and still more at the ridiculous idea of a boy writing for twelve voices, and exclaimed: "O, you silly youngster! are not two voices sufficient for you?" These curt rebuffs were profitable to Haydn. Reutter advised him to write variations to his own liking upon the pieces he heard in church, and this practice gave him fresh and original ideas which Reutter corrected. "I certainly had talent, and by dint of hard work I managed to get on. When my comrades were at their sports, I went to my own room, where there was no danger of disturbance, and practiced," says Haydn.

Dies, speaking further of this time in Haydn's youth, says: "I must guess at many details, for Haydn always spoke of his teacher with a reserve and respect which did honor to his heart"—feelings all the more to his credit when we consider the following statements, from the same authority: "What was very

2

embarrassing to him and at his age must have been painful, was the fact that it looked as if they were trying to starve him, soul and body. Joseph's stomach observed a perpetual fast. He went to the occasional 'academies,' where refreshments were provided as compensation for the choir-boys, and once having made this valuable discovery, his propensity to attend was irresistible.   He tried to sing as beautifully as he could that he might acquire a reputation and thus secure invitations which would give him the opportunity of appeasing his gnawing hunger."   At such times, when not observed, he would fill his pockets with " nadeln " or other delicacies.   Reutter himself had very little income from which to pay his choir-boys, so they had to famish.

Notwithstanding he sensitively felt the misery of his condition, Haydn's youthful buoyancy did not desert him. Dies says : " At the time the court was building the Summer Palace at Schonbrunn, Haydn had to sing there with the church musicians in the Whitsuntide holidays.   When not engaged in the church he joined the other boys, climbing the scaffolding and made considerable noise on the boards.

One day the boys suddenly perceived a lady; it was Maria Theresa herself, who at once ordered some one to drive away the noisy youngsters, and threaten them with a whipping if they were caught there again. On the very next day, urged on by his temerity, Haydn climbed the scaffolding alone, was caught and received the promised punishment which he deserved. Many years afterward, when Haydn was engaged in Prince Esterhazy's service, the Empress came to Esterhaz. Haydn presented himself and offered his humble thanks for the punishment received on that occasion. He had to relate the whole story, which occasioned much merriment."

At that time we behold our hero in an exalted and dignified position, but how thorny was the upward course!

" The beautiful voice with which he had so often satisfied his hunger, suddenly became untrue and commenced to break," says Dies. The Empress was accustomed to attend the festival of St. Leopold at the neighboring monastery of Klosternenburg. She had already intimated to Reutter, in sport, that Haydn " could not sing any more, he crowed."

At this festival, therefore, he selected the younger brother, Michael, for the singing. He pleased the Empress so much that she sent him twenty-four ducats. As Haydn was no longer of any service to Reutter in a pecuniary way, and particularly as his place was now filled, he decided to dismiss his superfluous boarder. Haydn's boyish folly accelerated his departure. One of the other choir-boys wore his hair in a queue, contrary to the style, and Haydn had cut it off. Reutter decided that he should be feruled. The time of punishment came. Haydn, now eighteen years of age, sought in every way to escape, and at last declared that he would not be a choir-boy any longer if he were punished: "That will not help you. You shall first be punished and then march."

Reutter kept his word, but he counseled his dismissed singer to become a soprano, as they were very well paid at that time. Haydn, with genuine manliness, would not consent to the tempting proposal, and late in the autumn of 1749 he started out in the great world in which he was such a stranger, " helpless, without money, with three poor shirts and a threadbare coat." After wandering about the streets, distressed with hunger, he threw himself down on the nearest bench and spent his first night in the damp November air, under the open heavens. He was lucky enough to meet an acquaintance, also a choir-singer, and an instructor as well. Though he and his wife and child occupied one small chamber, he gave the helpless wanderer shelter—a trait of that Austrian humanity which, at a later period, was reflected in the exquisite tones of Haydn's art. "His parents were very much distressed," says Dies again; "his poor mother, especially, expressed her solicitude with tearful eyes. She begged her son to yield to the wishes and prayers of his parents and devote himself to the church. She gave him no rest, but Haydn was immovable. He would give them no reasons. He thought he expressed himself clearly enough when he compressed his feelings into the few words: 'I can never be a priest.'" In his seventy-sixth year, he said to the choir-boys who were presented to him: "Be really honest and industrious and never forget God." It is evident, therefore, that it was not the lack of sincere

piety that kept him from the priesthood.   He
felt that he was called to another and more
fitting sphere, and we now know that his feelings and impulses did not deceive him.

Necessity, however, came near forcing him
into the life he had so resolutely refused, for
he got little money from the serenades and
choir-work in which he took part, though at
other times it left him the wished-for leisure
for study and composition.   The quiet loneli
ness in that little dark garret under the tiles,
the complete lack of those things which can
entertain an unoccupied mind, and the utter
piteousness of his condition, at times led him
into such unhappy reveries that he was driven
to his music to chase away his troubles.   "At
one time," says Dies, "his thoughts were so
gloomy, or more likely his hunger was so
keen, that he resolved, in spite of his prejudices, to join the Servite Order so that he
could get sufficient to eat.   This, however,
was only a fleeting impulse, for his nature
would never allow him to really take such a
step.   His disposition happily inclined to joyousness and saved him from any serious out-
breaks of melancholy.   When the summer

rain or the winter snow, leaking through the cracks of the roof, awoke him, he regarded such little accidents as natural, and made sport of them."

For some time he was not positively sure what course to pursue, and he projected a thousand plans, which were abandoned almost as soon as they were formed. For the most part hunger was the motive that urged him on to rash resolves, for instance, a pilgrimage to the Maria cloister in Styria. There he went at once to the choir-master, announced himself as a chapel-scholar, produced some of his musical sketches, and offered his services. The choir-master did not believe his story and dismissed him, as he became more importunate, saying: "There are too many ragamuffins coming here from Vienna, claiming to be chapel-boys, who can't sing a note." Another day, Haydn went to the choir, made the acquaintance of one of the singers and begged of him his music-book. The young man excused himself on the ground that it was against the rules. Haydn pressed a piece of money into his hand and stood by him until the music commenced. Suddenly he seized the book

out of his hands and sang so beautifully
that the chorus-master was amazed, and afterward apologized to him. The priests also inquired about him and invited him to their
table. Haydn remained there eight days, and,
as he said, filled his stomach for a long time
to come, and afterward was presented with a
little purse made up for him.

Among the bequests in Haydn's will of
1802 is the following: " To the maiden, Anna
Buchholz, one hundred florins, because her
grandfather in my youth and at a time of
urgent necessity lent me one hundred and
fifty florins, without int "est, which I repaid
fifty years ago." This, for him a considerable
loan, enabled him for the first time to have a
room of his own where he could work quietly.
This was not far from the year 1750. Dies relates, in the year 1805: " Chance placed in
Haydn's hands, a short time before, one of his
youthful compositions which he had utterly
forgotten—a short four-voiced mass with two
obligato soprano parts. The discovery of
this lost child, after fifty-two years of absence,
was the occasion of true joy to the parent.
' What particularly pleases me in this little

work,' said he, 'is its melody and positive youthful spirit,' and he decided to give it a modern dress." The mass was by this means preserved ard may be regarded as his first large work. We are thus enabled to date it at the beginning of the year 1750.

At that time Haydn lived in the Michaeler house (which is still preserved), in the Kohl-market, one of the choicest sections of the city, but was again under the roof and exposed to the inclemency of the weather. At one time the room had no stove, and winter mornings he had to bring water from the well, as that in his wash-basin was frozen. There were some distinguished occupants in the house; the princess Esterhazy, whose son, Paul Anton, became Haydn's first patron, and the famous and talented poet Metastasio, who not long after confided to him his little friend Marianna Martines as a piano scholar, and paid his board as compensation. The child must have been well grounded in music, for thirty years later Mozart frequently played four-handed pieces with her. Her instruction, after the style of the time, obliged Haydn to write little com-positions. These early pieces circulated freely

but they have all been lost. He considered it
a compliment for people to accept them, and
did not know that the music-dealers were doing
a flourishing business with them. Many a
time he stopped with delight before the windows to gaze at one or another of the published
copies. That this work, however, was very
distasteful to him is evident from his own
words: "After my voice was absolutely gone,
I dragged myself through eight miserable
years, teaching the young. It is this wretched
struggle for bread which crushes so many men
of genius, taking the time they should devote
to study. It was my own bitter experience
and I should have accomplished little or nothing if I had not zealously worked at night
upon my compositions." Urgent as his necessity was, he declined to take a permanent
and good paying position in a Vienna band,
and thereby sell his entire time. "Freedom!
what more can one ask for?" said Beethoven.
Haydn insisted upon having it at least for his
genius. Many times in his life he gave expression to this feeling. In his old age he said to
Griesinger: "When I sat at my old worm-
eaten piano, I envied no king his happiness."

We shall see that he had more of real inward happiness as a composer, than as a pianist.

With such a disposition he easily retained his good humor and equanimity, and many of his youthful traits clearly reflect the Haydn of the genial minuets and humorous finales. For the entertainment of his comrades, who were never lacking, he once tied a chestnut roaster's hand-cart to the wheels of a fiacre, and then called to the driver of the latter to go on, while he quietly made off, followed by the curses of the two victims. At another time he conceived the idea of inviting several musicians at a specified hour to a pretended serenade. The rendezvous was in the Tiefengraben, where Beethoven lived for a few years after his arrival in Vienna. They were instructed to distribute themselves before different houses and at the street-corners. Even in the High Bridge street, where Mozart lived at a later period, stood a kettle-drummer. Very few of the musicians knew why they were there, and each had permission to play what he pleased. Dies concludes his description of this roguish trick as follows: "Scarcely had the horrible concert begun when the astonished occupants threw open their windows and commenced to curse the infernal music. In the meantime the watchmen approached. The players scampered off at the right time, except the drummer and one violinist, who were arrested. As they would not name the ringleader, they were discharged after a few days' imprisonment."

It was at this time of his early struggles that he went out one day to purchase some piano work suitable for study, and acting upon the advice of the music-dealer took a volume of the sonatas of Philip Emanuel Bach, the composer, who first placed piano music upon an independent and so to speak, poetical foundation. "It appears to me," says this gifted son of the great Bach, in an autobiographical sketch, "that it is the special province of music to move the heart." To such an one the genial and imaginative nature of our genuine Austrian musician did involuntary homage from the very first. "I never left my piano until I had played the sonatas through," said Haydn, when old, with all the enthusiasm of youth, "and he who knows me thoroughly can not but find that I owe very much to Bach, for I understood and studied him profoundly. Indeed, upon

one occasion he complimented me upon it."
Bach once said that he was the only one who
completely understood him and could make
good use of his knowledge. Rochlitz informs
us that Haydn said: "I played these sonatas
innumerable times, especially when I felt troubled, and I always left the instrument refreshed
and in cheerful spirits." A sketch of this
same Bach, dated 1764, says: "Always rich
in invention, attractive and spirited in melody,
bold and stately in harmony, we know him already by a hundred master-pieces, but not as
yet do we fully know him."

In reality, instrumental music was now for
the first time entering with self-confidence and
strength upon the freer path of the opera. The
end of that path, though far distant, was individual characterization. Bach himself once
wrote a preface to a trio for strings. He says
in it that he has sought to express something which otherwise would require voices
and words. It may be regarded as a conversation between a sanguine and a melancholy
person who dispute with one another through
the first and second movements, until the melancholy man accepts the assertion of the other.

At last, they are reconciled in the finale. The
melancholy man commences the movement
with a certain feeble cheerfulness, mixed with
sadness, which at last threatens tobecome actual grief, but after a pause, is dissipated in a
figure of lively triplets. The sanguine man
follows steadily along, " out of courtesy," and
they strengthen their agreement, while the one
imitates the other even to his identity. From
such germs, in which the intellectual idea is more
than its artistic expression, Haydn evolved that
which made him the founder of modern instrumental music, the extreme limit of which is the
representation of the world's vital will.

Melody, in other words, the vital will illu-
minated by reason, also begins at this point to
assert its sure mastery, as the song and the
dance were then the essential type of this modern instrumental music. Key, accent, rhythm,
even the rests, now became the conscious
means of fixed color and tone, in which every
emotion, every aspiration, every exertion of
our powers has its full value. Harmonic modulations help to maintain and to deepen the
given tone-color. Above all else, the dissonance is no longer a matter of mere chance or

transient charm to the ear, but the road to an absolute effect, designed by the composer. Bach many a time sought for it, but Haydn gave it poetical effect. He does not hesitate, for example, in the finale of the great E flat major sonata, to introduce the augmented triad, which Richard Wagner uses in such a strikingly characteristic manner, bringing it in as a prepared dissonance, but at the same time allowing it to enter freely. And still more, they had before them the boundless treasures of Sebastian Bach, which Mozart and Beethoven at a later period opened so fully and which they emphasized with such heart-stirring power.

The difference of keys moreover became recognized as of greater value, and the ground-color of pieces is more individual. It does not follow, however, on this account that the marvelous gifts of native counterpoint were thrown aside. On the other hand, Haydn, in his treatment of the so-called thematic development in the second part of the first movement and in the finale of the sonata, brings them out according to their proper intellectual value, so that this music also must be "heard with the understanding." Finally, the salient

points of the whole style, which was called the
"galante," because it did not belong to the
church or to the erudite but to the salon, is
as, we may say, the grand architectural gra-
dations and building up of the whole, which
gives to it an arrangement of parts like the
symmetry of the Renaissance art, and the
same similarity modern music in general holds
to the Gothic of the German counterpoint.
Haydn by nature and every vital function, belonged to active life, with its manifold forms
of thought and changing mental conditions,
and, therefore, found the sonata-form the very
best for the depositing of his musical wealth,
and for the magnifying of his own inner powers and capacities by its further development.
It was for this reason that he played the Bach
"Sonatas for Students and Amateurs" with
such delight and sat at his piano so gladly, for
it aroused in him a freer activity of fancy and
heart-felt emotions of similar form.

Philip Emanuel Bach's instruction book,
the "Versuch uber die wahre Art das Clavier
zu spielen," published in Berlin in 1753, with
which Haydn became acquainted shortly afterward, was, in his judgment, "the best, most

thorough and useful work which had ever appeared as an instruction book," and Mozart as well as Beethoven expressed the same opinion, and yet the ridiculous accusation was made after this that Haydn had copied and caricatured Bach, because Bach was not on good terms with him. The story may perhaps have arisen from the fact that Bach in his autobiography (1773) sought to attribute the decline of the music of his day to "the comedian so popular just now." This, however, referred to something entirely different, and in 1783, Bach publicly wrote: "I am constrained by news I have received from Vienna to believe that this worthy man, whose works give me more and more pleasure, is as truly my friend as I am his. Work alone praises or condemns its masters, and I therefore measure every one by that standard." Dies even declares that Haydn, in 1795, returned from London by way of Hamburg to make the personal acquaintance of Bach, but arrived too late, for he was dead. Bach died in 1788, and could it be possible that Haydn was not aware of it? The journey by way of Hamburg had another purpose.

3

Haydn still kept up his violin practice, and received further instruction from his countryman and friend, Dittersdorf, afterward the composer of "The Doctor and Apothecary." Dies says: "Once they strolled through the streets at night and stopped before a common beer-house, in which some half drunk and sleepy musicians were wretchedly scraping away on a Haydn minuet. 'Let us go in,' said Haydn. They entered the drinking-room. Haydn stepped up to the first fiddler and very coolly asked: 'Whose minuet is this?' The fiddler replied still more coolly, and even fiercely: 'Haydn's.' Haydn strode up to him, saying with feigned anger: 'It is a worthless thing.' 'What! what! what!' shrieked the interrupted fiddler, in his wrath, springing up from his seat. The rest of the players imitated their leader, and would have beaten Haydn over the head with their instruments, had not Dittersdorf, who was of larger stature, seized him in his arms and shoved him out of doors."

Dittersdorf himself, in his biography, narrates another instance of this intimacy. In 1762, he accompanied Gluck to Italy. During his absence, the famous Lolli appeared in Vienna with great success. On his return, he resolved to surpass Lolli's fame, and feigning sickness he kept his room for an entire week, and practiced incessantly. Then he reappeared and achieved a success. The universal verdict was, that Lolli excited wonder and Dittersdorf too, but that the latter played to the heart also. He adds: "The rest of the summer and the following winter, I was frequently in the society of the gracious Haydn. Every new piece of other composers which we heard we criticised between ourselves, commending what was good and condemning what was bad."

But let us return to the year 1750. Dies says: "When about twenty-one years of age, Haydn composed a comic opera with German text. It was called 'Der Krumme Teufel,' ('The Devil on Two Sticks') and originated in a singular way. Kurtz, a theatrical genius, was at that time the manager of the old Karnthnerthor theater, and amused the public as *Bernardon*. He had heard Haydn very favorably mentioned, which induced him to seek his acquaintance. A happy chance soon fur-

nished the opportunity. Kurtz had a beautiful wife, who condescended to receive serenades from the young artists. The young
Haydn (who called this 'Gassatim gehen,'
and composed a quintet for just such an oc-
sion in 1753) brought her a serenade, whereat
not only the lady but Kurtz also felt honored.
He sought Haydn's closer acquaintance, and
after this, the following scene occurred in his
house. 'Sit down at the piano,' said Kurtz,
 and accompany the pantomime which I will
perform for you, with fitting music. Imagine
that *Bernardon* has fallen into the water and
is trying to save himself by swimming!'
Kurtz calls an attendant and sprawls across a
chair, while it is drawn here and there about
the room, flinging out his arms and legs like
a swimmer, Haydn meantime imitating the
motion of the waves and the action of swimming in $\frac{6}{8}$ time. *Bernardon* suddenly sprang
up, embraced Haydn, and, nearly smothering
him with kisses, exclaimed: 'Haydn, you
are the man for me. You must write me an
opera! This was the origin of 'Der Krummè
Teufel.' Haydn received twenty-five ducats
for it, and thought himself very rich. It was

brought out twice with great applause and was then prohibited on account of the offensive personality of the text."

Here, therefore, we have an example of the fruitful germs of invention which Haydn displayed in motives and melodies, showing us, as it were, a personal presence possessing those musical characteristics which Mozart and Beethoven developed with such striking fidelity to life, and which by their efforts again invested dramatic representation with a new language. What the Italian had accomplished only in the way of a certain native grace of melody, and the French, on the other hand, with too partial a study in their dramatic recitative and piano music, German intelligence, and above all, German feeling, accomplished by the unprejudiced acceptance of melody itself. We also observe, mingled with these elements, that vein of German humor which first welled up in complete spontaneity and fullness in Haydn's music, so that we have, as it were, all the successive steps of development in the building up of his artistic individuality. At this point his youth and the main part of his early education close. We have reached the period of his first original creation, but it may be of interest, before we close this first chapter, to add a few words about the opera itself, in order that we may appreciate the real nature of this first original accomplishment of the artist as it deserves.

We observe, first of all, that in the test of his skill he was to illustrate a storm at sea and the struggle of a drowning man, and that Haydn's fingers at last involuntarily fell into the movement, ($\frac{6}{8}$ time), which the comedian wished. In the piece itself, an old, love-sick dotard was to be be cured and the good-natured devil must help. The details of this story and many other incidents of that period of art in Vienna may be found in C. F. Pohl's "Joseph Haydn," Vol. I (Berlin, 1875). But the principal point to be observed here is the close union of absolute music with the dramatic element, especially with the action, and that it was the perfection of the genuine humor of the popular Vienna comedies of that time which first directed Haydn's fancy to the expression of pantomime in tones. When the "Krumme Teufel" was finished, Haydn brought it to Kurtz, but the maid would not let him in, so

we are told, because her master was "study-
ing." What was Haydn's astonishment when
looking through a glass door he beheld *Bernardon* standing before a large mirror, making
faces and acting comical pantomime ! It was
the "free, sprightly comedy" which the Vienna harlequin possessed, and which was now
revealed to Haydn in its complete individuality by personal observation. But finally, while
this humor was kept down at this time by its
own crudeness and narrowness, as soon as the
higher dramatic poetry of the German language sprung up in Austria, it reappeared in
a nobler form in music, and it is Haydn who
represented this genuine German popular humor in our art. The last Vienna harlequin,
Bernardon, and his buffoonery disappeared,
but the comedy was preserved in full and permanent inheritance by Haydn in his comic
opera, "Der Krumme Teufel." The opera itself we do not possess, but its healthy and noble promise is realized all through Haydn's
instrumental music, to the origin of which we
now come.

CHAPTER II.

AT PRINCE ESTERHAZY'S.

Haydn's Studies with Porpora—His Italian Operas—Engagement with Count Von Morzin—His First String Quartet—An Unfortunate Marriage—Domestic Troubles without End—Appointment as Capellmeister at Esterhaz—His Orchestra and Chorus—Rapid Musical Growth—His Most Important Earlier Compositions—Development of the Quartet—Personal Characteristics and Anecdotes—The Surprise Symphony—Influence of his Life at Esterhaz upon his Music.

"His hours were occupied with lesson-giving and studies. Music so far monopolized his time that at this period no other than musical books came into his hands. The only exceptions were the works of Metastasio, and these can hardly be called an exception, as Metastasio always wrote for music, and therefore a Capellmeister who had determined to try his powers in opera ought to have been acquainted with his writings," says Dies. We know from Haydn himself that an Italian singer and opera composer was his last instructor in thor-

(40)

ough-bass; and that he had composed much but was not firmly grounded, that is, was not correct and strong until he had the good fortune to study the fundamental principles of composition, with the famous Porpora.

The Neapolitan, Nicolo Porpora was in Vienna from 1753 to 1757. He belonged to that early school of Italian opera which dominated nearly all Europe. The charm of melody predominated at this time and with it, the art of singing. They had reached their highest point. Smoothly flowing melody, however, was considered the main essential, and above all things, clearness and very simple harmonic structure characterized this school. Haydn played the accompaniments when Porpora gave singing lessons to the ten-year-old Martines and to the mistress of an ambassador, and was paid with lessons in composition from the impetuous and supercilious old master. " Ass, vagabond, blockhead," alternating with blows, greeted this not very accomplished " Tedesco" (German). For three months he filled the position of servant and blacked his master's shoes. " But I improved in singing, in composition and in Italian very much," says the modest mechanic's son, who, plain and simple himself, loved his art above all else. In fact, compared with the German music before him, or even with Philip Emanuel Bach's sonatas, Haydn's style at once shows not only that he had abandoned the "Tudesk" (German), of which the Italians complained, but that he had obtained a more refined phrasing of melody and a greater clearness of harmony, whereas the art of Bach had not advanced beyond the intellectual and characteristic. He also gave up embellishments and manifested a strong desire for the pure lines, and above all recognized that symmetry of construction which was rare among the Germans themselves, and yet constitutes an essential feature of modern German instrumental music.

The first larger works of Haydn were also Italian operas. He prized them very much himself, and they were also very pleasing to others; and it was only a deep, inward feeling for the calling he had chosen and a happy chance, which gave him the opportunity of satisfying that feeling, that saved him from a course which certainly might have secured him speedy fame and fortune, but not that immor-

tal halo of glory which crowns the " Father of
the Symphony." He even declined an invitation from Gluck, at that time the most celebrated of the Italian opera-composers, to go to
Italy! Apart from this, it may be said inci-
dentally, we learn of no nearer relations between
these two artists. Temperament, character and
the objects of their ambition kept them widely
apart.

Haydn now devoted himself still more earnestly to studies of a theoretical nature. From
sixteen to eighteen hours daily work was his
rule, two-thirds of the time being devoted to
the necessities of life. Mattheson's "Voll-
kommener Capellmeister" and the " Gradus
ad Parnassum " of Fux, the Vienna Hofcap-
pellmeister, were his text-books. "With un-
wearied determination Haydn sought to master the theory of Fux," says Griesinger, the
councilor, who met him frequently in 1800,
and in 1810 published the "Biographical Notices" of him. He says : " Haydn studied out the
problems, laid them aside some weeks, then
looked them over again and reviewed them
often enough to make sure he was master of
them Haydn called this work (" Fux's The-

orie "), a classic, and kept a much worn copy
of it all his life.   Mattheson's book was found
among his relics, " completely gone."   This
work certainly did not extend his knowledge
of composition, but he prized the method, and
educated many a scholar in it during his life,
and among those scholars was—Beethoven.

" He officiated as organist at a church in the
suburbs, wrote quartets and other pieces which
commended him still more favorably to amateurs, so that he was universally recognized as
a genius," says Dies.   One of these amateurs
was the councilor, Von Furnberg, "from whom
I received special marks of favor," says Haydn
himself.   Von Furnberg, who was already indebted to Haydn for several trios, was accustomed to have chamber-music at his villa in
Weinzerl, played by the pastor of the place,
his own steward, a violoncellist, and Haydn,
and one day encouraged the latter to write a
string quartet.   Thus an accident of his surroundings turned his inventive spirit toward
that particular form of chamber-music, the
string-quartet, which was destined to be so
wonderful in results.   This occurred in 1750.

Much had been already written for the four

stringed instruments, but Haydn gave to the quartet the movements and organic form which he had found in the sonatas. By the force of his knowledge of harmony he gave a more spontaneously melodious capacity to the divisions of the quartet which had hitherto been merely vague and sketchy, so that their development captivated the player and listener. It was, as it were, a scene in which four individualities, acting together, play out a complete and concrete life-picture,—artistic performances, which appeal to the player, as well as to the artist and poet, in a higher degree than the simple, plain sonata. Hence the invention of the string-quartet marked an epoch in the history of music.

The first quartet (B flat, $\frac{6}{8}$), met with such an instant success and so actively inspired Haydn himself, that in a short time he produced eighteen works in this style. And yet a Prussian major who had been made a prisoner in the Seven Years' War, who heard these early productions, says that although every one was in raptures over his compositions, Haydn was modest even to timidity, and could not bring himself to believe that they were of any account. Twenty years later, even, he looked up to Hasse, at that time indeed famous throughout the world, as a great composer, and declared he would treasure his praise of his "Stabat Mater" like gold, though it was undeserved, "not on account of the opinion itself, but for the sake of a man so estimable." Who knows Hasse to-day, and who that knows anything of music is not familiar with Joseph Haydn and his quartets? The English musichunter, Burney, mentions that in 1772 he heard them played at Gluck's!

It contributed greatly to his activity in composition that he was now in better circumstances. Furnberg had secured for him the appointment of "director" in the establishment of a music-loving count. The first quartets breathe the full, joyous humor of his child-like spirit. Though at first many a one protested against the lowering of music to mere trifling and was of the opinion that there was no earnest effort in his compositions, the verdict this time declared itself in favor of the creator of this style, and many a deeply earnest tone in these works is a souvenir of happy hours, which even now a quartet-evening with Haydn affords.

The Count, who in 1759 had installed Haydn as his director—and one in that position must also be a composer—was the Bohemian nobleman, Franz von Morzin. He passed his winters in Vienna and his summers at his country house at Lukavec, where he kept his orchestra, and while with him Haydn wrote his first symphony. There were symphonies indeed long before Haydn. Originally, all music in several parts was thus designated—at first, vocal pieces with instrumental accompaniments, but after the seventeenth century, instrumental music only. The instrumental preludes to the Italian operas, in particular, were called symphonies. The symphony in regular form consisted of an Allegro, an Adagio and a second Allegro. Haydn made the three movements, which he had transferred from the sonata-form to the quartet, richer and more independent, and added to them the Minuet, so that four movements became the rule. Haydn's progress, therefore, was exemplified in the symphony by the freedom and vivacity which he gave to the separate instruments, but above all, by their

skillful combination and the dynamic grada-
tions of the ensemble. For these he had his
models in the compositions of the Mannheim
school, which Mozart so much admired afterward.

Haydn's first symphony, in D major, is a
prominent example of the clearness of his
method in such larger orchestral work. We
shall soon see that he developed it still farther. His position with the Count, satisfactory so far as compensation was concerned,
might have been the source of prolific creation, for the Count and his young son were
enthusiastic musical amateurs, but the contract
stipulated that he should remain unmarried.
Haydn was then twenty-seven years of age,
and it was not until that time that the charms
of the other sex attracted his attention, and it
happened then only by an accident which reveals to us the innocence of his youth. In
his later years he was fond of telling the story
that once when he was accompanying the young
Countess in her singing, she stooped over, so as
to see better, and her neckerchief became dis-
arranged. "It was the first time I had ever
witnessed such a sight. I was embarrassed,

my playing ceased, and my fingers lay idly on the keys," he told Griesinger. "What has happened, Haydn," said the Countess, "what are you doing?" With perfect respect, Haydn replied: "Who could retain his self-command in your gracious ladyship's presence?" The sequel to such an unexpected revelation was not long in following.

In the autumn of 1760, Haydn was again with his scholars in Vienna. Among them were two daughters of Keller, a wig-maker, in the Ungargasse, who had frequently assisted him before this time. The younger daughter was so attractive to him, that in spite of the Count's order, which only made her still more alluring to the fiery young fellow, he determined to marry her, but to his sorrow, she chose to enter a convent. "Haydn, you ought to marry my eldest daughter," jokingly said the father one day, for he was particularly pleased with the smart and gifted young director;—and Haydn did so. Whatever may have been the reason—gratitude, ignorance, helplessness in practical matters, or the wish to have a wife right away—whatever may have

4

been the motive, he married, and sorely he had to suffer for it.

His wife was older than he, and this of itself made the relations between them very uncertain. Besides this, Dies says that she was an imperious and unfeeling woman, who was incapable of any consideration, and had earned the reputation of being a spendthrift. The proofs of her quarrelsomeness and of her heartless treatment of her husband reveal to us a perfect Xantippe. As compared with the simple, frank and joyous-hearted Haydn, she was an extreme bigot and prude. Only a person of his disposition could have endured such a wretched, and above all, childless marriage. "We were affectionate together, but for all that, I soon discovered that my wife was extremely frivolous," he very mildly said to Dies. He told Griesinger that he was obliged to carefully conceal his earnings from her on account of her passion for finery. She was also fond of inviting priests to dine, urging them to say many masses, and giving more money to them for charity than she could afford. Very many of Haydn's masses, and smaller church-pieces, especially those scattered about

in the Austrian convents, are due to. the fact
that she availed herself of her husband's talent
to appear generous. Under such circumstances
he naturally did not accomplish his best work,
but wrote in a careless style.   Once, when
Griesinger, for whom he had done some favor
for which he would not accept anything, asked
permission to make his wife a present, he resolutely replied: "She does not deserve anything.
It is little matter to her whether her husband is
an artist or a cobbler."   She was also particularly malicious, and purposely tried to offend
her husband, using his notes, for instance, as
curl-papers, and in pie dishes, occasioning the
loss, undoubtedly, of many of his earlier scores.
One day, when she complained that there was
not money enough in the house to bury him,
in case he died suddenly, Haydn called her
attention to a row of canons which were framed
and hung upon the wall of his chamber, in lieu
of any other decoration, and told her that they
would bring enough for his funeral expenses.
Notwithstanding his patience and good-heart-
edness, he could not overcome an intuitive feeling of repugnance for his wife. In the year
1805, when the violinist Baillot was visiting

him, they happened to pass a picture in the hall. Haydn stopped, and grasping Baillot by the arm, said: "That is my wife. Many a time she has maddened me."

Is it not natural, then, and excusable also, that at times he sought solace away from home? * * * An Italian singer, in particular, Luigia Polzelli, won his affections in later years, and bestowed upon him a loving sympathy. He writes to her from London in 1792, thirty-two years after his unfortunate marriage, in furious terms: "My wife, *bestia infernale*, has written so much stuff, that I had to tell her I would not come to the house any more, which has brought her again to her senses." A year later he says, in a gentler and almost sorrowful tone: "My wife is ailing most of the time and is always in the same miserable temper, but I do not let it distress me any longer. There will sometime be an end of this torment." The remark in Lessing's "Jungere Gelehrten," "I am obliged to admit that I have had no other aim than this: to practice those virtues which enable one to endure such a woman," exactly apply to Haydn's case. At last he could bear it no

longer.   He procured board for her with the
teacher Stoll, at Baden, who is spoken of in
Mozart's letters, and she died there in 1800.
Haydn dearly earned that exquisite peace
which characterized so many of his adagios,
but it was the true rest of the soul, and it is
only here and there that a softly sighing chord
reminds us of Wotan's words: "The victory
was won through toil and trouble from morning until night."   The unrestrained outpour-
ings of love Haydn could not express.   When
Adam and Eve in " The Creation," or Hann-
chen and Lucas sing their fond strains, you
never think of Constance and Pamina, and yet
Haydn wrote both these works long after Mozart was dead.   The fullness and dignity of
true womanly nature, in which his own wife
was wanting, he was elsewhere to learn and
value, as we shall yet see.   The tenderer and
deeper notes of the heart are not wanting in
his compositions; on the contrary, he was the
first to introduce them in music in all their
perfection.

   We now resume the course of our narrative.
Dies says: " Six months passed by before
Count Morzin knew that his Capellmeister

was married.   Circumstances occurred which
changed Haydn's affairs.   It became necessary
for the Count to reduce his large expenses and
to dismiss his musicians, and thus he lost his
position."   Prince Esterhazy, however, a short
time before, had become acquainted with some
of his orchestral pieces and admired them.
His growing fame, his admirable personal
character, besides Morzin's hearty commenda-
tions, secured for him the position of Capellmeister to the Prince in the same year (1761),
and he held it nearly to the close of his life.
This position settled Haydn's future as a composer.

The Esterhazy residence is in the little town
of Eisenstadt, in Hungary, where the Prince's
castle supplied accommodation for every style
of musical and dramatic performances.   Music
in particular had been patronized by the family for many generations.   Here, in undis-
turbed quiet, Haydn actively devoted himself
to those remarkable compositions which de-
servedly proclaim him the founder of modern
instrumental music.   The Prince had a pretty
complete orchestra, though it was small, and a
modest chorus, with two soloists.   It was also

expected' that the servants and attendants, after
the custom of that time, would assist as musicians. The entire force of musicians was
placed under the direction of the new Capellmeister, who was raised to an official position.
By virtue of his rank, he was obliged to appear daily in the antechamber and receive instructions with regard to the music. He was
also expected to compose what music was
necessary and drill the singers. His contract
of May 1, 1761, commends the duty required
of him to his skill and zeal, and hopes that he
will keep the orchestra up to such a standard
as will reflect honor upon him and entitle him
to further marks of princely favor.

Rarely, indeed, has a hope been more fully
realized. The orchestra was soon a superior
one, and it was not long before the works written for it by Haydn became famous throughout the world. The very first of the Esterhazy symphonies in C major, known as "The
Noon," showed that he was determined to
bring the Prince as well as the orchestra to a
realization of the work before them. It makes
demands upon the orchestra which this one
could not supply till much later, as it was

written in a very large and broad style. It
also has in it a foreshadowing of Beethoven's
dramatic style, in a recitative for violin with
orchestra, introduced in one movement. He
himself was also more thoroughly grounded in
his own artistic work. The ever increasing
interest which the Prince took in him (to
Paul Anton, succeeded the next year, Nicholas, Anton following him in 1790, and a second
Nicholas following Anton in 1795) was a fresh
incentive to his creative talent, so that the
confinement in his rural situation during the
twenty years that he passed with the first two
Princes did not weigh very heavily upon him.
After 1766, he spent many of the winter
months with his Prince in Vienna. "My
Prince was always satisfied with my works. I
not only had the encouragement of steady ap-
probation, but as leader of the orchestra, I
could experiment, observe what produced and
what weakened effects, and was thus enabled to
improve, change, make additions or omissions,
and venture upon anything. I was separated
from the world, there was no one to distract or
torment me, and I was compelled to become
original." Such a statement as this, which

was made to Griesinger, shows what an important influence his life at this period had upon his artistic development.

There are many other interesting details of this Esterhazy life.   Griesinger says :   "Fishing and hunting were Haydn's favorite pleasures during his stay in Hungary."   Think for a moment what an influence such an unbroken, restful life in God's free nature must have had upon him, especially when it is considered that this had continued for thirty years and had been his only recreation outside of his own profession.   " The dew-dropping morn, O how it quickens all," says Eve in " The Creation."   In the early morning, the best time for his favorite pleasure, when the sun rose, shining in its full splendor, " a giant proud and joyous," or at evening the moon " stole upon " the home-returning hunter with " soft step and gentle shimmer," how his heart must have expanded as the sublime solitude of Nature revealed itself to him and spoke its own language !   It was a time when the sense of nature rose superior to all the artifices of custom, and her majesty and chaste purity made a deep impression upon every noble feeling.

In this sacred solitude, which with his beloved
art filled his life with its only happiness and
contentment, he stripped off his powdered wig
and stood up clothed in his own pure manhood.   What the result was may be seen in
his exuberant melodies, earnest as well as passionate, which picture the innocent joy of
Nature.

Many other things he learned to picture at
this time.   It was only that free and appre-
ciative contemplation of Nature, which continual intimate intercourse with her produces,
which enabled him to keenly observe the characteristics of every one of her phenomena and
to give them conscious expression in his old
age, in "The Creation" and "The Seasons."
The "Noon" symphony was soon followed by
the "Morning."   That he intended to express
in this music the "awakening of impressions
upon arriving in the country," is shown by a
concerto which appeared soon afterward, "The
Evening," and which closes with a storm.   According to Dies, his Prince had commissioned
him to make the divisions of the day subjects
for composition.   We know by their reception that these works revealed an entirely new

world of music. Beethoven, with his incomparably deeper feeling for Nature, received his first impulses of that feeling from this music. The original can only be found in Haydn's quiet life at Eisenstadt with Prince Esterhazy. We shall find further confirmation of the influence of this life in the following details:

The bearing of Prince Nicholas, then in his fortieth year, corresponded with his surroundings. Rich and distinguished as he was, he had noble passions. His appearance at Court was brilliant, while the richness of his jewels was proverbial. But his love of art and science was far greater than his fondness for show and court display, and in true Hungarian fashion, music was the dearest of all to him. He was a genuine Austrian cavalier of the best old times. Goodness of heart, magnanimity and kindly feeling were his prominent traits of character, and he manifested these qualities especially toward his orchestra. " During the entire period of his rule, his records, nearly all of which begin with the declaration, ' God be with us,' are a continuous series of releases from moneyed as well as other obligations, and rarely was a request refused," says Pohl, in his reliable biography of Haydn. Still he could be severe without retaining animosity. His own instrument was the baryton, at that time very much admired, which has long since been superseded by the noble violoncello. Apropos of this instrument, the following characteristic event occurred:

The Prince played only in one key. Haydn practiced for six months, day and night, upon the instrument, often disturbed by the abuse of his wife, and upon one occasion incurred the censure of the Prince for neglecting his compositions. Thereat, impelled by a fit of vanity, he played upon the instrument at one of the evening entertainments in several keys. The Prince was not at all disturbed, and only said: "Haydn, you ought to have known better." At first he was pained by the indifference of his honored master, but he immediately felt it was a gentle reproof, because he had wasted so much time and neglected his proper work to become a good baryton player, and turned to his compositions again with renewed earnestness. For the baryton alone, he has written upwards of one hundred and seventy-five pieces.

Haydn's real feelings towards the Prince are shown by his words in his autobiography of 1776:—"Would that I could live and die with him." Upon the accession of the new administration, his salary was increased one-half, and afterward six hundred florins were added, besides which he received frequent gifts from the Prince. This helped to appease his longing to go abroad, particularly to Italy—a longing which many a time must have arisen in his solitude. He recalled, even in his old age, with grateful feelings the good and generous Prince Nicholas, who had twice rebuilt his little house after it had been reduced to ashes by fires in the city. Though he wrote much, very much, simply for the Prince's personal gratification, and consequently much that had little value, yet the Prince's knowledge of music was sufficient to realize Haydn's constant development and to actively foster it. Haydn was not under personal restraint, at least not more than was customary in a court at that time of "literal, primitive despotisms." Though he was not the less a courtling, he remained an artist, and clove to his own rank. " I am surrounded by emperors, kings and many exalted persons, and I have had much flattery from them, but I will not live upon familiar terms with them; I prefer the people of my own station," he said to Griesinger. In his later years, indeed, he personally asserted his dignity before his Prince and master. On his return from London, he bitterly complained because he was addressed by the customary "Er," as an inferior, and after that he was always called " Herr von Haydn," and " Respected Sir," or " Dear Capellmeister von Haydn." Upon one occasion the young Prince Nicholas expressed his disapproval of a rehearsal, and Haydn replied: " Your Highness, it is *my* duty to attend to these matters." A glance of displeasure was the only response of His Highness.

With the orchestra itself, which numbered many excellent players, Haydn had trouble many a time. The easy lenity of the Prince made it careless, and what the habits of musicians were at that time Mozart's biography shows. " The appeals of Haydn are touching and heart-reaching when he intercedes for those who have erred only through careless- ness," says Pohl. He also helped to appease the Prince with specially arranged composi- tions. To these probably belongs the sym- phony in five movements, called " Le Midi," with a recitative for the first violinist, Toma- sini, who was a special favorite of the Prince— a proof that the images of his fancy were al- ready influencing him, and that, like Gluck, he was determined not to be "a mason," but an "architect." That he put his whole soul into these compositions is shown by the inscrip- tions at the beginning and end—" In nomine Domini," " Laus Deo," etc.

His most important compositions during his earlier years at Esterhaz were Italian operas. The Prince had engaged foreign actors, and the festival occasions at the palace, which as we know were often attended by royal per- sonages, were made brilliant by these theat- rical performances. During his thirty years stay at Esterhaz more than a dozen of these works were brought out, some of which Haydn himself esteemed. They certainly show a copious richness of detail, of harmonic beauty and of instrumental effects. " When Cheru-

bini looked through some of my manuscripts,
he always hit upon places which were deserving
of attention," said Haydn to Griesinger, and
Cherubini, at that time an opera composer *par
excellence*, might well be concerned about the
superiority of Haydn's operas. But the
qualities which were conspicuous in Haydn's
instrumental music, the sure movement of the
whole work and the freedom of the intellectual
development, were wanting in his operas.
This was Gluck's contribution to the opera.
Haydn had no part in it. He recognized
himself that his operas in originality of form
could scarcely equal those of Gluck in the
more modern period. And yet we shall find
that one of his operas was performed in
London.

A criticism in the *Vienna Zeitung* during
the year 1766 gives us another picture of his
varied acquirements and of his successful activity as well as of the character of his genius.
He is enumerated among the distinguished
composers of the imperial city at that time under the title of "Herr Joseph Haydn, the
favorite of the nation, whose gentle character
is reflected in every one of his pieces. His

compositions possess beauty, symmetry, clearness, and a delicate and noble simplicity, which impress themselves upon the listener even before he has become specially attentive. His quartets, trios and other works of this class are like a pure, clear strip of water, ruffled by a southern breeze, quickly agitated and rolling with waves but preserving its depth. The doubling of the melody by octaves originated with him and one can not deny its charm. In the symphony, he is robust, powerful and ingenious; in his songs, charming, captivating and tender; in his minuets, natural, merry and graceful."

One can see that in all his leading qualities Haydn was recognized in his own time. Rigid masters, like Haydn's predecessor in service, the Capellmeister Werner, a genuine representative of the old contrapuntal school, were freely at hand with such epithets as " fashionhunter " and "song-scribbler." But the acute Berlin *Critic*, at that time hostile to everything South German, declared of Haydn's quartet, op. 19, and the symphony, op. 18, that they displayed the most "original humor and

5

sprightly agreeable spirit." It is J. F. Reichardt who says this: "Never," says he, "has
there been a composer who combines so much
unity and variety with so much agreeableness
and popularity. It is extremely interesting
to consider Haydn's works in their successive
order. His first works, twenty years ago, showed that he had an agreeable humor of his own,
and yet it was rather mere pertness and extrav-
agant mirth, without much harmonic depth.
But by degrees his humor became more manly
and his work more thoroughly considered,
until through elevated and earnest feeling, ri-
per study, and above all, effect, the matured,
original man and trained artist were manifest."
"If we had only a Haydn and Philip Emanuel
Bach, we Germans could boldly assert that we
have a style of our own, and that our instrumental music is the most interesting of all," he
says in conclusion.

Haydn had also transferred to the richer
string quartet and full orchestra, the sonata-
form founded by Philip Emanuel Bach, the
organic character of which is shown by the
theory and history of music. How he developed this form in its final perfection it is not

necessary to consider in detail at this time. He established, as we know, its four-part form in the Allegro, Adagio, Minuet and Finale, and by his great productivity and popularity brought this form into universal use. He was the first to give to the Minuet, which is attractive in itself, a popular, genial, and above all, a cheerful, humorous spirit. He very materially broadened, arranged and elevated the first movement of the sonata-form, gave to it more fullness and meaning through the organic development of its own motive substance, deepened the Adagio from a simple song (cavatina), to a completely satisfying tone-picture, and above all, by thematic treatment, produced in the Finale the veritable wonders of the mind and of life. That Haydn greatly heightened the effect of the symphony by giving to the various instruments their full development is apparent at once in his music, and yet it should not be forgotten that Mozart, who had studied the performances of the orchestras at Mannheim and Paris, also influenced him, above all in his operas. But the crowning result of Haydn's work will always remain the germ of active life which he im-

parted to this form, and which he developed so
freely that it presented a definite and finished
shape.   Haydn first gave the quartet and symphony that style which may be called its own.

Philip Emanuel Bach's "Sonatas for Students and Amateurs," always have something
which may be called studied about them.
They are thoughtful and considered, above all
skillful and intellectual; but the free expression
of feeling only appears at intervals, especially
in the Adagio where Bach could depend for
his effect upon the operatic aria and the feeling of the original German Lied.   The great
Sebastian Bach's instrumental works are cy-
clopean structures, pelasgic monuments, often
the elementary mountains themselves. Many
a time there looks out of the stone, as it were,
a visage, but it is a stony-face, like that on the
Loreley or the romantic Brocken--apparition:
"And the long rocky noses, how they snore,
how they blow."   They are stone giant-bodies,
mighty Sphynx-images, which conceal more
than they tell.   In the sharpest contrast with
this music was the opera of that time, in which
fashionable puppets affected an outward, stilted
appearance of dramatic activity.   Gluck first

stripped off the gaudy tinsel and revealed the concealed earnestness of the reality. The instrumental music of the French and Italians suffered also from this affectation and superficiality of the theatrical music, and Scarlatti, Corelli and Couperin made the utmost effort to restore the free expression of feeling and unrestrained nature to their own place in music.

He who first revealed this "natural," this inborn, and therefore spontaneous art, in music, speaking through its own nature and with its own voice, was our Haydn, and it was for this that Beethoven called him great and posterity has called him immortal. And, as the Italians say, that no man can paint a more beautiful head than he has himself, so, though we have seen this Haydn physically and intellectually, what matters it, if his portrait appears to us reversed in his music?

Haydn was slender but strong, and below the medium height, with legs disproportionately short, and seeming all the shorter, owing to his old-fashioned style of dress. His features were tolerably regular, his face serious and expressive, but at the same

time attractive for its benignity. " Kindliness
and gentle earnestness showed themselves in
his person and bearing," says Griesinger.
When he was in earnest, his countenance was
dignified, and in pleasant conversation he had
a laughing expression, though Dies says he
never heard him laugh aloud. His large
aquiline nose, disfigured by a polypus, was,
like the rest of his face, deeply pitted by small-
pox, so that the nostrils were differently shaped.
The under lip, which was strong and somewhat coarse, was very prominent. His com-
plexion was very brown. One of his biographical sketches mentions that he was called a
Moor. He considered himself ugly, and mentioned two Princes who could not endure his
appearance, because he seemed deformed to
them. He stuck to his wig, which has been
already mentioned, in spite of all the changing
modes, through two generations, even to his
death, but it concealed, to the disadvantage of
the general expression of his physiognomy, a
large part of his broad and finely developed
forehead. Lavater, looking at his silhouette,
said: " I see something more than common in
his nose and eyebrows. The forehead also

is good. The mouth has something of the Philistine about it."

"There was great joyousness and mirth in his character," says Dies, and in his old age he said himself: "Life is a charming affair." Joy in life was the fundamental characteristic of his existence and his compositions. His individual lot and his satisfaction with common things contributed to this. "Contentment is happiness," says the philosopher. The unvarying simplicity of his life secured him the luxury of good health, and next to that, the feeling of joy in living. But in reality it is not this life-joyousness alone that is reflected in his works. Though the influence of his outward life and of his inner development were conducive to quiet reflection and earnest thought, he preferred to give a sprightly turn to conversation. We have already learned how deep were his personal attachments and gratitude. He was also very beneficent and kindly disposed. "Haydn's humanity was exhibited to the high and low," Dies once said, and modesty was his simple Austrian virtue. Griesinger justly attributes religion as the basis of all these qualities, which

with him was the simple piety of the heart—
not a mere passing impulse, but the All and
the Eternal reflected in him. The result of
this beautiful influence upon him was that he
was never imperious or haughty, notwithstanding all the fame that was so profusely
showered upon him during his life. "Honor
and fame were the two powerful elements that
controlled him, but I have never known an
instance," says Dies, "where they degenerated
into immoderate ambition." He regarded his
talent as a blessed gift from Heaven, and no
one was more ready to give new comers their
just deserts. He always spoke of Gluck and
Handel with the most grateful reverence, just
as he did of Philip Emanuel Bach. Of his
incomparably beautiful relations with Mozart
we shall soon learn. Nevertheless he was not
ignorant of his own worth. "I believe I have
done my duty, and that the world has been
benefited by my works. Let others do the
same," he used to say. He could not endure
personal flattery and when it was offered
would resent it. He never allowed his goodness to be abused and if it were attempted
he would grow irritated and satirical.

"A harmless waggishness, or what the English call humor, was a leading trait in Haydn's character. He delighted in discovering the comical side of things, and after spending an hour with him you could not help observing that he was full of the spirit of the Austrian national cheerfulness," says Griesinger. We may well conceive that in his younger days he was very susceptible to love, and in his old age he always had compliments for the ladies; but we must understand his remark that "this is a part of my business," in the same sense that Gœthe's "Elegie Amor" is "stuff for song," and the "higher style" to the romantic poets. In fact, without some such personal inspiration, like the ever-glowing and universal fire that animates humanity, many of his pieces, especially his adagios, can not be understood. "It has a deep meaning; it is rather difficult, but full of feeling," he once said of a sonata, to his highly esteemed friend, Frau von Genzinger, whom we shall soon meet. It is the one, according to all the indications, which the letters give, whose Adagio Cantabile is in B sharp major, ¾, and has in the second part a

grand and mystical modulation, with shifting
of melody in the treble and bass by means of
the crossed hands. The first Allegro is also
constructed like a quiet conversation between
a male and female voice. "I had so much to
say to Your Grace and so much to confess,
from which no one but Your Grace could
absolve me," he writes. He begs that he
may call her a friend "for ever," and the
Minuet, which she had asked of him in a
letter a short time before, wonderfully expresses the request.

At a later period in London, he took an
English singer, Miss Billington, under his
protection, whose conduct was not highly regarded and had even been severely criticised
in the public press. "It is said that her character is faulty, but in spite of all this, she is a
great genius, though hated by all the women
because she is handsome," he writes in his
diary. The diary also contains letters from
an English widow, Madame Schroter, who
loved him devotedly. "She was still a beautiful and attractive woman, though over sixty,
and had I been free, I should certainly have
married her," he said upon one occasion to

Dies, with his peculiar roguish laugh. A single extract from these tender letters is enough for us to understand the depth of her devotion: - " My dearest Haydn, I feel for you the deepest and warmest love of which the human heart is capable." Unless it has something to feed upon, however, the hottest fire will be extinguished. He could not comprehend in his later life, how so many beautiful women had fallen in love with him. " My beauty could not have attracted them," he said in 1805, to Dies, and when the latter replied, " you have a certain genial something in your face," he answered: " One may see that I am on good terms with every one." " He did not fancy that he was made of any better material, nor did he seek, through assumed purity, to place himself on any higher plane of morality than his own opinion justified," explains Dies. He was the unaffected child of his Austrian home in a time when one seemed still to wander in Paradise and life had no thorns.

Thus, from every point of view, Joseph Haydn stands before us an original, well defined personality, passing, as his life-long bearing shows us, from an artificial and unnatural time in every way, to a period of the renewed free assertion of individuality and its involuntary expression of feeling. He tells us with the utmost naivete, that it was not composition but inclination and enthusiasm that had been his inspiration. "Haydn always sketched out his works at the piano," says Griesinger. "I seated myself and began to compose," says Haydn, whatever my mood suggested, sad or joyous, earnest or trifling. As soon as I seized upon an idea, I used my utmost efforts to develop and hold it fast in conformity with every rule of the art. The reason why so many composers fail is that they string fragments together. They break off almost as soon as they have commenced, and nothing is left to make an impression upon the heart." He always wrote, impelled by inspiration, but at first only the outlines of the whole. That it was this poetico-musical impulse that urged him on, is shown by the following anecdote:

"About the year 1770, Haydn was prostrated with a burning fever, and his physician had expressly forbidden him to do any musical work during his convalescence," says Grie-singer. "His wife shortly afterward went to church one day, leaving strict instructions with the servant about the doctor's orders. Scarcely had she gone, when he sent the servant away upon some errand, and hurriedly rushed to the piano. At the very first touch the idea of a whole sonata presented itself in his mind, and the first part was finished while his wife was at church. When he heard her coming back he quickly threw himself into bed again and composed the rest of the sonata there. Mozart and Beethoven certainly did not at first need the piano in composing, and it is by no means certain that Haydn also did not find that first movement in bed. In any case, the anecdote shows the simple, artistic, involuntary power that moved him."

From the same source also proceeded the vital personal impulse of his joyous expression, and the individual physiognomy of the themes and motives in his compositions. His melody throughout reminds one of the aria, not in the affected rococo style of Louis Fourteenth's time, but based upon grammatical

declamation; and it is only a certain regularly
recurring pattern of the melody that makes us
feel it belongs to the very time in which he
was living.   The separate parts of the sonata-
form were infused with a stronger vitality by
this virile humor and elevated and refined
feeling.   In this connection Griesinger's remark is specially pertinent.   "This humor is
extremely striking in his compositions, and
this is specially characteristic of his Allegros
and Finales, which playfully keep the listener
alternating from what has the appearance of
seriousness to the highest style of humor, until it reaches unrestrained joyousness."   Dies
calls it "popular and refined, but in the
highest sense, original musical wit."   This
musical frolicsomeness opened in reality a new
and richly profitable province for art.   It
aroused a spirit which had hitherto slumbered,
and from Mozart and Beethoven, even to
Schumann and Wagner, we find this simplest
soul-voice and these wonderfully expressive
tones, ravishing and at the same time sorrowful in their nature, springing up; for the
basis of this voice is the involuntary but deep
feeling for human life, sorrowing with its

sorrow, merry with its folly, and always intimately associated with all human actions.

Haydn himself attributes to this state of
mind many features of his Adagios as well as
of his Minuets and Finales. The increasing
intellectual progress brought in time " ideas
which swept through his mind and which he
strove to express in the language of tones."
He himself told Griesinger that in his symphonies he often pictured " moral attributes."
In one of the oldest the prominent idea was
that God spoke to a hardened sinner, beseech-
ing him to repent, but the careless sinner gave
no heed to the admonition. A symphony of
the year 1767 is called " The Philosopher ; "
a divertimento, " The Beloved Schoolmaster; "
and another work of a later period, " The
Distracted One."

An anecdote of the year 1772 shows us a
characteristic illustration of this artistic life-
work. After the year 1766 the Prince made
a summer-residence of the castle at Esterhaz,
on the Neusiedler-See, where he remained
fully half the year, accompanied by the best
of his musicians. " I was at that time young
and lively, and consequently not any better off

than the others," said Haydn with a laugh, especially in reference to the longing of his musicians to go home to their wives and children. "The Prince must have known of their very natural home-sickness for some time, and the ludicrous appearance they presented when he announced to them that he had suddenly decided to remain there two months longer, amused him very much," says Dies. The order plunged the young men into despair. They besieged the Capell-meister, and no one sympathized with them more than Haydn. Should he present a petition? That would only expose them to laughter. He put a multitude of similar questions to himself, but without answer. What did he do? Not many evenings after, the Prince was surprised in a very extraordinary manner. Right in the midst of some passionate music one instrument ceased, the player noiselessly folded up his music, put out his light and went away. Soon a second finished and went off also; a third and fourth followed, all extinguishing their lights and taking their instruments away. The orchestra grew smaller and more indistinct. The

Prince and all present sat in silent wonder. Finally the last but one extinguished his light, and then Haydn took his and went also. Only the first violinist remained. Haydn had purposely selected this one, as his playing was very pleasing to the Prince and therefore he would be constrained to wait to the end. The end came. The last light was extinguished and even Tomasini disappeared. Then the Prince arose and said, "If all go, we may as well go too." The players meanwhile had collected in the anteroom, and the Prince said smiling, "Haydn, the gentlemen have my consent to go to-morrow." It was the composition which afterward became well known under the name of "The Surprise Symphony."

In like manner Haydn through his music, so to speak, could reduce his ideas and emotions to practical reality. The Chapter of the Cathedral at Cadiz desired some music for Good Friday which should follow at the end of and complete the interpretation of the Seven Words of the Savior on the Cross, after they had been spoken and explained by the priest. Haydn himself says in a letter to London, that

6

any text of the nature of the Seven Words can only be expressed by instrumental music; that it made the deepest impression upon his mind; and that he justly esteemed it as one of his best works. It was performed twice at a later period in London under his own direction. In the Finale he has an earthquake effect, which was called for the third time at his own benefit concert there, and is the precursor of the imagery of "The Creation." The work as a whole is of decidedly characteristic quality. This was in the year 1780 and that Haydn was selected for the work, shows not only how far his fame had extended at that time, but above all, that his artistic ability to invest instrumental music with the gift of language was unmistakably recognized. Thus the master's art was firmly established abroad, and he did not have to wait long before grander themes of larger proportions were tendered him.

We close with a selection of characteristic expressions made by Haydn in these earlier years of his work, about his art and artistic progress, most of which are to be found in the "Musical Letters."

In the year 1776, he says in that autobiography which was requested of him for a " Learned National Society " in Vienna, that in chamber-music he has had the good fortune to please almost all people except the Berliners. His only wonder was that " these judicious Berlin gentlemen " kept no medium in their criticisms, at one time elevating him to the stars, and at another " burying him seventy fathoms deep in the earth," and this without any good reason. But he knew the source of all these attacks upon his artistic work.

The Vienna Pensions Verein for artists' widows which to-day bears the name of Haydn, and for which he had written the oratorio " The Return of Tobias," stipulated as a condition of his admission to membership, that besides the above work, he should bind himself to furnish some composition every year for the benefit of the Society, and in case of failure to do so should be dismissed. Haydn at once demanded his deposit back, and addressed them in the following manner : " Dear friends, I am a man of too much feeling to constantly expose myself to the risk of being cashiered. The free arts and the beautiful science of composi-

tion can endure no fetters upon their handi
work. *Heart and soul must be free !* "

This was in the year 1779. It marks the
full development of his artistic consciousness.
He was more and more convinced of the lofty
mission of an art which has its source in such
creations. In the year 1781, he expressed the
wish to have the opinion of the Councilor
Von Greiner, one of the most distinguished
connoisseurs in Vienna, often mentioned in
Mozart's biographies, with regard to the expression of his songs, and assures his publisher,
Artaria, that for variety, beauty and simplicity,
they excel any other he has written. The
French admired exceedingly the pleasing
melody of his " Stabat Mater," work of that
kind not having been heard in Paris, and very
rarely indeed in Vienna. This is all the more
remarkable, as Gluck at that time had already
written and brought out his great dramatic
works collectively. Some of his songs had
been " wretchedly " set to music by the Vienna
Capellmeister Hoffmann, Haydn goes on to
relate, and as this swaggerer believed that
he alone had scaled Parnassus, and sought to
crush Haydn down in certain circles of the

great world, he had set the same songs to show
this pretended great world the difference.
"They are only songs, but not Hoffmannish
street-songs, without ideas, expression, and
above all, melody," he closes. We can no
longer doubt from this that he would not
suffer his creations to be despoiled of their
spiritually-poetic nature. He would not allow
his songs to be sung by any one until he himself had brought them out in the concert-
room. "The master must maintain his rights
by his own presence and correct performance,"
says he. It is this distinctive nature and form
of modern music which is fully revealed for
the first time in Mozart and Beethoven, and
music which has been created by the intellect
can only be properly judged by the intellect.

There was also that inner something, "the
musical nature," which impelled him and
urged him on to his most characteristic creations. "One is seized upon by a conscious
mood which will not endure restraint," he
once said. In like manner at another time he
made the characteristic remark: "The music
plays upon me as if I were a piano." Apropos of the technical side of music, he char-

acteristically remarked to Dies in 1805: "If an idea struck me as beautiful and satisfactory to the ear and the heart, I would far rather let a grammatical error remain than sacrifice what is beautiful to mere pedantic trifling."

Finally, that we may point out to the player some instances of this actual life-painting in tones, let us take the well known Peters' Edition, which is easily accessible to every one. First of all, among the thirty-four piano sonatas, the one in C sharp minor is a beautiful piece of earnest work and full of character, the Minuet very melancholy and illustrating the national melody of that southern people. No. 5 is the clearest picture of buoyant health. One can see young life at play in the spring-meadows. In No. 7 the music assumes a strange capriciousness, and in the Largo in D minor, notwithstanding it is barely eighteen measures long, shows the grand tragic style of Beethoven, as well as its humor, which recalls the variations in F minor, whose color and rhythm suggest the funeral march in the Eroica. The Adagio of the A flat major sonata, No. 8, is a gem of the intellectual development of all harmonic and

contrapuntal means, and in the Larghetto of
No. 20, surely all the nightingales of life are
deliciously warbling. Both of these are complete lyric scenes. Above all, the first as well
as the last sonata of Haydn's shows a plastic
touch, which clearly reveals this master's natural and artistic feeling, and often fills us with
overwhelming astonishment at the power of
genius, which in such small limits and with
such simple means can utter things that to-
day are immediately recognized, wherever
feeling exists and is capable of manifesting
itself in the comprehension of the mission of
human life.

Richer, greater, more inwardly finished,
if not always esthetic in the highest sense
throughout, this appears in the quartets,
and here, above all else, we first discover that
Haydn in that style was the forerunner of Mozart and Beethoven alike, and still further, that
he was the original source of the success of the
later Italians who copied his sprightliness, his
thoughtful style, amiability and natural spirit,
while the German heroes found their native
power and their free mental conception and
method in his own inner life, culminating

in the matchless melody of Franz Schubert.
These spirited first movements, these flowing
Finales, these Minuets, these Adagios, full of
ever-increasing and exuberant wit, how irre-
sistibly they seize upon one! How their warm
affection satisfies! It is, in fact, "Idea, Expression, Melody." Glance only at the pieces
which may be found in the Peters' Edition:
Op. 54, with the highly characteristic Minuet
and the Finale, is remarkable in itself
for a Presto contained in the Adagio, as well
as for being the precursor of the Adagio of
Beethoven's sonata, op. 31, No. 1. The Adagios in op. 74, op. 76 and op. 77, are still
grander in tone, but not more beautiful or
fervent than those of op. 54 and op. 64. The
Adagio in op. 103 has in its concluding measures somewhat of the blessed and elevated
nature of the close of that most beautiful of all
soul-poems which pure music has created,—
the Lento of op. 135, Beethoven's grave-song.
We need not mention the symphonies, those
well known works of Haydn. Everywhere
in his music we meet what Goethe calls the
absolute source of all life—"Idea and Love."

We have seen that isolation enriched and

prospered Haydn. We arrive now at a period when by his intimate personal association with Mozart, and his entrance into the great changing outer world, he was destined to develop his genius to its fullest extent.

CHAPTER III.

A Winter Adventure—The Relations of Mozart and Haydn—
Mozart's Dedication—The Emperor Joseph's Opinions—
Letters to Frau von Genzinger—A Catalogue of Com-
plaints—His Engagement with Salomon—The London
Journey—Scenes on the Way—A Brilliant Reception—
Rivalry of the Professional Concerts—The Händel Festival—
Honors at Oxford—Pleyel's Arrival—Royal Honors—His
Benefit Concert—Return to Vienna.

" I am already at home in Vienna by my
few works, and if the composer is not there
his children always are in all the concerts,"
replied Haydn to that Charity for artists' widows, which wished to elect him as a " foreigner," upon such severe conditions.   We meet
with a characteristic instance of this popularity about the year 1770, when he once, as was
his habit, went to Vienna on business.

It was winter.   Over his somewhat shabby
garments he had thrown a fur cloak, whose
age was also conspicuous.   An uncombed wig

and an old hat completed his costume. Haydn, so great a friend of neatness, on this occasion would hardly have been recognized. He looked like a masquerader, when he entered Vienna. At the residence of a Count in Karnthner Street he heard the music of one of his own symphonies. The orchestra was powerful, the players good. "Stop, coachman, stop." Haydn sprang out of the carriage, hurried up to the house, ascended the steps, entered the vestibule and listened quietly at the door. A servant approached, surveyed the strange apparition from head to foot, and at last thundered out: " What are you doing here, sir?" " I would like to listen a little." " This is no place for listening; go about your business." Haydn pretended not to hear the abuse. The servant at last seized him by the cloak with the words: " You have heard enough, now pack off or I will pitch you out doors." Haydn handed him a couple of Kreuzer pieces. As soon as the Allegro was finished the servant again urged him to go. Haydn wanted to hear the Adagio, and was searching his pocket anew, when by chance the door was opened, and he was recognized by one of the players. In an instant the hall resounded with a loud greeting. "Haydn, Haydn," was on every lip! The doors were thrown open and more than twenty persons surrounded the revered master and bore him into the salon, a part of them greeting him as an acquaintance and the rest seeking an introduction. In the midst of the loud acclamation, a shrill voice above them cried out: "That is not Haydn; it is impossible. Haydn must be larger, handsomer and stronger, not such a little insignificant man as that one there in the circle." Universal laughter ensued. Haydn, more astonished than any of the rest, looked about him to see who had disputed his identity. It was an Italian Abbe who had heard of Haydn and admired him very much. He had mounted a table in order to see him. The universal laughter only ended with the commencement of the Adagio but Haydn remained until the close of the symphony.

"My only misfortune is my country life," Haydn writes in the spring of 1781, but he could be in Vienna two of the winter months at least, and there it was he found the artist,

who more than all others, not excepting even
Philip Emanuel Bach, influenced him and
helped to raise his fame " to the stars "—
Mozart.

Their personal acquaintance first commenced in the spring of 1781, when Mozart
came to Vienna and permanently remained
there. The letters of Mozart's father, during
the journeys of 1764 and 1768, make no mention of Haydn, and in the summer of 1773,
when Mozart passed a short time in Vienna,
Haydn as usual was at Esterhaz. Mozart's
own letters however show that even as a boy
he knew and admired Haydn. He sent for
his Minuets from Italy, and also created a taste
for the German Minuet among the Italians.
The actual acquaintance between these two
artists, so widely apart in years, the true foundation of which both in life and in their works,
rested above all upon that cordiality which is
so intimate a part of German life, must have
brought them very closely together. How
Mozart felt towards Haydn, a statement of
Griesinger's shows. Haydn once brought out
a new quartet in the presence of Mozart and
his old enemy, the Berliner, Leopold Kozeluch,

in which some bold changes occurred. "That sounds strange. Would you have written that so ?" said Kozeluch to Mozart. "Hardly" was the reply, "but do you know why? Because neither you nor I could have hit upon such an idea." At another time, when this talentless composer would not cease his fault-finding, Mozart excitedly exclaimed : "Sir, if we were melted down together, we would be far from making a Haydn."

Association with the circles, in which at this golden time of music in Vienna, Haydn's compositions were cherished with pleasure and love, and even with actual devotion, by artists and connoisseurs, inspired him to accomplish something of equivalent value. As early as the autumn of 1782, he commenced to write a series of six quartets, and the Italian dedication of them to Haydn is the most beautiful instance of unselfish admiration that can be conceived. It was written in the autumn of 1785, and the translation reads :

My dear friend Haydn:

When a father sends his sons out into the wide world, he should, I think, confide them to the protection and guidance of a highly celebrated man, who by some happy dispensation is also the best among his friends. So to this famous man and most precious friend, to thee, I bring my six sons. They are, it is true, the fruit of long and laborious toil, but the hope which my friends hold out to me leads me to anticipate that these works, a part at least, will compensate me, and it gives me courage and persuades me that some day they will be a source of happiness to me. You, yourself, dearest friend, expressed your satisfaction with them during your last visit to our capital. Your judgment above all inspires me with the wish to offer them to you, and with the hope that they will not seem wholly unworthy of your favor. Take them kindly, and be to them a father, guide and friend. From this moment I resign all right in them to you, and beg you to regard with indulgence the faults which may have escaped the loving eyes of their father, and in spite of them to continue your generous friendship towards one who so highly appreciates it. Meantime I remain with my whole heart, your sincere friend.

W. A. MOZART.

He called Haydn " Papa," and when some one spoke of his dedication, replied: " That was duty, for I first learned from Haydn how one should write quartets." How Haydn with his simple modesty always bowed to divinely inspired genius, is shown by a letter from Mozart's father, of the fourteenth of February of the same year, 1785, which may be found complete in the book : " Mozart, after Sketches by his Cotemporaries," (Leipsic, 1880). It reads : " On Saturday evening Herr Joseph Haydn was with us. The new quartets were played, which complete the other three we have. They are a little easier but delightfully written. Herr Haydn said to me : 'I declare to you, before God and upon my honor, your son is the greatest composer with whom I am personally acquainted. He has taste and possesses the most consummate knowledge of composition.'" That was truly an expression of " satisfaction," and to such a " father " Mozart might well entrust his " children." He understood their merits and character. " If Mozart had composed nothing else but his quartets and his ' Requiem ' he would have been immortal," the Abbe Stadler heard Haydn remark afterwards. During a discussion of the well-known discord in the introduction to the C major quartet, he declared that if Mozart wrote it so, he had some good reason for it. He never neglected an opportunity of hearing Mozart's music, and declared that he could not listen to one of his works without learning something. Kelly in his Reminiscences, tells of a quartet performance about the year 1786, in which Haydn, Dittersdorf Mozart and Banhall took part—certainly an unprecedented gathering. Dittersdorf, of whose virtuoso playing mention has already been made, must have played the first violin.

In the year 1787, "Don Juan" was brought out in Prague, and as Mozart could not entertain a proposition for a second opera, application was made to Haydn. He wrote from Esterhaz, in December, one of the most beautiful of all his letters. It is contained in Mozart's Biography : "You desire a comic opera from me," he says. " Gladly would I furnish it, if you desired one of my vocal compositions for yourself alone, but if it is to be brought out in Prague, I could not serve you, because all my operas are so closely connected with our personal circle at Esterhaz, and they could not produce the proper effect which I calculated in accordance with the locality. It would be different, if I had the inestimable privilege of composing an entirely new work for your theater. Even then, however, the risk would be great, for scarcely any one can bear compari-

7

son with the great Mozart.   Would that I
could impress upon every friend of music, and
especially upon great men, the same deep sympathy and appreciation for Mozart's inimita-
ble works that I feel and enjoy ; then, the na-
tions would vie with each other in the possession of such a treasure.   Prague should hold
fast to such a dear man, and also remunerate
him, for without this the history of a great man
is sad indeed, and gives little encouragement
to posterity for effort.   It is for the lack of
this, so many promising geniuses are wrecked.
It vexes me that this matchless man is not yet
engaged by some imperial or royal court.
Pardon me if I am excited, for I love the
man very dearly."

The above reproach was superfluous so far as
Mozart was concerned, for he had at that time
been appointed chamber-composer at the imperial court, though Haydn, being in Eisenstadt, did not know it; but without any doubt
the reproach was applicable in another case—
that of Haydn himself.   The recognition of
his special work had as yet made but little
progress among the professional musicians,
critics and influential circles.   His letters are

full of protests against this injustice and misfortune, and the statements of Mozart, already
quoted, show how just they were. The elegant leaders of Italian fashion and Spanish
etiquette were not more likely to encourage a
low-born Esterhaz Capellmeister in uncivilized
Hungary than they were the national humor,
pleasantry and vivacity which had for the first
time found proper expression in music, and
the liberties which these qualities permitted,
contrary to the accepted style, were either not
recognized at all, or looked upon as mistakes.
It was all the more unfortunate for him that
Joseph II was the very embodiment of this
foreign manner. The well known Reichardt,
who met the Emperor in Vienna in 1783, relates: "I thought at least in a conversation
about Haydn, whom I named with reverence,
and whose absence I regretted, we should
agree. 'I thought,' said the Emperor, 'you
Berlin gentlemen did not care for such trifling.
I do n't care much for it, and so it goes pretty
hard with the excellent artist.'" This in a
measure is confirmed by a conversation between Joseph and Dittersdorf, two years later:
"What do you think of his chamber-music?"

"That it is making a sensation all over the world, and with good reason." "Is he not too much addicted to trifling?" "He has the gift of trifling without degrading his art." "You are right there."

While such malicious partiality and miscomprehension must have distressed Haydn very much, it secured for him the renewed good opinion of Mozart and recognition of his elevated character, and he did not refrain from giving expression to it. "It was truly touching when he spoke of the two Haydns and other great masters. One would have thought he was listening to one of his scholars rather than to the all-powerful Mozart," says Niemetscheck, speaking of Mozart's visit to Prague. Rochlitz also reports the following opinion which Mozart expressed: "No one can play with and profoundly move the feelings, excite to laughter and stir the deepest emotions, each with equal power, like Joseph Haydn." Such reverence must have given the master the fullest conviction of his artistic power, for who was better qualified to pass such judgment than such a genius? Meanwhile this judgment was confirmed by unprejudiced hearers all over the world. As we learn from Gyrowetz's Autobiography, a sym- phony of this young master was played in Paris as a favorite composition in all the theaters and concerts, because it was mistaken for a work of Haydn's. He also had to spe- cially protect his music from being clandes- tinely copied and engraved.

It is not surprising therefore to hear him say at the close of a letter in 1787, in which he offers a London publisher the " Seven Words," six " splendid " symphonies, and three " very elegant " nocturnes : " I hope to see you by the close of this year, as I have not yet received any reply from Herr Cramer as to an engagement for myself this winter in Naples." The London invitation concerned the so-called professional concerts. A year afterward, J. P. Salomon contracted with him for concert-engagements in the Haymarket theater. Mozart writes to his father in 1783 as follows : " I know positively that Hofstetter has twice copied Haydn's music," and Haydn himself in 1787 writes to Artaria : " Your own copyist is a rascal, for he offered mine eight ducats this winter to let him have the

'Seven Words.'" He justly complains that he is not paid sufficiently for his works, and on one occasion thanks Artaria "without end for the unexpected twelve ducats." "I have until now kept it from my readers that Haydn declared on the occasion of my first visit to him he had been in straightened circumstances to his sixtieth year," says Dies, and he adds that in spite of all his economy and the generosity of Prince Nicholas at his death, and thirty years of hard toil, his entire property consisted of a small house and five hundred florins in gold. Besides this he had about two thousand florins in public funds which he had laid aside against a time of need. Dies rightly attributes such penury after such industry to the extravagance of his wife. But notwithstanding the Esterhazy goodness, the fact remains that Haydn often found himself longing for a change. It mattered little that he had equal fame with Gluck and Mozart. Such a Prince should have kept the purse of a man of such sensitive and exalted feeling well filled.

"My greatest ambition is to be recognized by all the world as the honest man which I

really am," he writes about the year 1776,
and dedicates all the praises he had received
"to Almighty God, for to Him alone are they
due." His wish was neither to offend his
neighbor nor his gracious Prince, and above
all, the merciful God. Now that he realized
the beautiful divine pleasure of reverence, and
that his unworthy situation with its constant restrictions and distress pressed upon his
artistic feeling, he longed for a change more
ardently than ever. "I had a good Prince,
but at times had to be dependent on base
souls; I often sighed for release," he writes
from London in 1791. His determination to
accept the London invitation must have been
very strong, for a letter of 1781 closes:
"Meanwhile I thank you very much for the
lodgings offered me." His gratitude actually
prevented him from traveling, though he was
literally besieged by his friends, and, as we
have seen, was invited from abroad. "He
swore to the Prince to serve him until death
should separate them and not to forsake him
though he were offered millions," Dies heard
him say. The Prince in times of pressing necessity allowed him to draw upon his credit,

but Haydn availed himself of this privilege as seldom as possible, and was always satisfied with small sums.

Among impressions so varied in their nature, the letters were written which belong to the following year and from which we must present a few short extracts. They are addressed to Frau von Genzinger in Vienna, the wife of a physician who was also physician in ordinary to Prince Esterhazy. She was very intimate with our master in his later years, for she had made his friendship in connection with his art, having arranged symphonies of his for the piano. In reading these letters, one truly feels the noble aspirations of Haydn's soul. The influence which this excellent lady had upon the poetical character of his works is evident in the beautiful sonata whose Adagio "meant so much." Here indeed vibrate accords as full of life and longing as music was capable of expressing at that time in her soft measures.

In the house of this "ladies' doctor," as he was universally called in Vienna, Mozart, Dittersdorf, Albrechtsberger, afterward Beethoven's teacher, and Haydn, when he was in Vienna, met regularly on Sundays, and it must have been doubly painful to him to go back to his wretched solitude from these delightful gatherings where he could sit near her ladyship and hear the master-pieces of Mozart played. Alas! the separation came sooner than Haydn wished. "The sudden resolution of my Prince to withdraw from Vienna, which is hateful to him, is the cause of my precipitate journey to Esterhaz," he writes in 1789. In contrast with the other magnates, who were fond of displaying their splendor and gratifying their tastes, and nowhere was this so true as in Vienna, Prince Nicholas with his increasing years grew more and more unpopular in that city. Haydn himself gives the most forcible expression to his dissatisfaction with his surroundings.

The address: "High and nobly born, highly esteemed, best of all, Frau von Genzinger," shows us the style of the time, and the following letter of February 9, 1790, tells us the whole story:

"Here I sit in my wilderness, deserted like a poor orphan, almost without human society, sad, full of the recollections of past happy days, yes, past, alas! And who can say when

those delightful days will return—those pleasant gatherings, when the whole circle were of
one heart and soul—all those charming musical evenings which can only be imagined, not
described?   Where are all those inspired moments ?   All are gone, and gone for a long
time," he writes, and it was only his native
cheerfulness that could allay this feeling of
loneliness.   " Wonder not, dear lady, that I
have delayed so long in writing my gratitude.
I found every thing at home torn up.   For
three days I was uncertain whether I was
Capellmeister or Capell-servant.   Nothing
consoled me.   My entire apartment was in
confusion.   My piano, which I love so much,
was inconstant and disobedient, and it vexed
instead of tranquilizing me.   I could sleep
but little, my dreams troubled me so.   When
I dreamed of hearing ' The Marriage of Fig-
aro,' a fatal north-wind awoke me and almost blew my night-cap off my head."   In
his next remarks we learn of a composition,
about which he had written a short time before to his publisher, saying that he had in
his leisure hours composed a new capriccio for
the piano, which by its taste, originality and

close finish would be sure to receive universal applause. " I became three pounds thinner on the way," he continues, " because of the loss of my good Vienna fare. Alas, thought I to myself, when in my restaurant I had to eat a piece of fifty-year-old cow instead of fine beef, an old sheep and yellow carrots instead of a ragout and meat balls, a leathery grill instead of a Bohemian pheasant! alas, alas, thought I, would that I now had many a morsel which I could not have eaten in Vienna! Here, in Esterhaz, no one asks me, 'Would you like chocolate? Do you desire coffee with or without milk? With what can I serve you, my dear Haydn? Will you have vanilla or pine-apple ice?' Would that I had only a piece of good Parmesan cheese, so that I might the more easily swallow the black dumplings! Pardon me, most gracious lady, for taking up your time in my first letter with such piteous stuff. Much allowance must be made for a man spoiled by the good things in Vienna. But I have already commenced to accustom myself to the country by degrees, and yesterday I studied for the first time quite in the Haydn manner."

An event shortly after occurred which
for the time greatly stimulated. his creative
ability. The Princess died, and the Prince
sank into such melancholy that he wanted
music every day. At this time he would not
allow him to be absent for twenty-four hours.
He speaks often of his deep distress of heart
and of his many disappointments and ill hu-
mors. " But, thank God, this time will also
pass away," he says at the close of a letter, in
which he is looking forward to the winter.
" It is sad always to be a slave, but Providence
so wills it," he says on another occasion. " I
am a poor creature, continually tormented
with hard work, and with but few hours for
recreation. Friends? What do I say? One
true friend? There are no longer any true
friends, save one, oh! yes, I truly have one,
but she is far away from me; I can take refuge, however, in my thoughts; God bless her
and so order that she shall not forget me."
" My friendship for you is so tender that it
can never become culpable, since I always
have before my eyes reverence for your
exalted virtue," he also wrote in reply to
Frau von Genzinger, concerning a letter
which to his regret had been lost.

We now come to a time when the "ill-humors" ceased, and Haydn secured a better situation, and, more than all, complete freedom. The Prince died and crowned his generosity with the legacy of a pension of one thousand gulden. The new Prince, Paul Anton, added four hundred gulden more to it, so that Haydn could now live comfortably upon a stipend of two thousand eight hundred marks. He discharged the orchestra and only required of Haydn that he should retain the title of Capellmeister at Esterhaz. Haydn called this position "poorly requited" and added that he was on horseback, "without saddle or bridle," but hoped one day or other by his own service, "for I can not flatter or beg," or by the personal influence of his gracious Prince, to be placed in a higher position. But this did not occur until a later time, and then by the help "of his fourth Prince." He soon removed to Vienna, and declined the invitation of Prince Grassalkowic to enter his service. It was not long before his affairs took a happy turn in another direction, and in the place of rural restraint he enjoyed the widest and most unrestricted public liberty.

The violinist, J. P. Salomon, a native of
Bonn, who had played in Haydn's quartets
long before and occupied a distinguished place
in the musical world of London, entered his
room one evening and curtly said: "I am Salomon, of London, and have come to take you
away. We will close the bargain to-morrow."
He was on his travels engaging singers for the
theatrical manager Gallini, and on his return
to Cologne, heard of the death of Prince Esterhazy. Haydn at first offered various objections—his ignorance of foreign languages, his
inexperience in traveling and his old age; but
Salomon's propositions were so brilliant that
he wavered. Five thousand gulden, and the
sale of his compositions were something worth
unusual consideration in the straightened circumstances of a simple musician, entering upon
old age. Besides, he had plenty of compositions finished which no one knew of outside
of Esterhaz. He made his assent conditional
upon the Prince's permission and gave no further heed to Salomon's persuasions. Mozart
himself, who had traveled much about the
world, interposed his objections with the best
intentions. "Papa" was too old. He was

not fitted for the great world. He spoke too few languages. A man of fifty-eight ought to remain quietly among his old and sure friends. " I am still active and strong, and my language is understood all over the world," he replied.

The Prince did not refuse his permission, and the expenses of the journey were advanced. Haydn sold his little house at Eisenstadt, took the five hundred gulden which he had saved up, consigned his bonds to his " highly cherished " Vienna friend to whom he commended his wife, and made all his preparations for the journey which was to establish his fame all over the world. He started Dec. 15, 1790. Mozart did not leave his beloved " Papa " the whole day. He dined with him, and tearfully exclaimed at the moment of separation: " We are saying our last farewell to-day." Haydn was also deeply moved. He was twenty-four years older, and the thought of his own death alone occurred to him. It was but a year later that he heard of Mozart's death, and shed bitter tears. " I shall rejoice in my home and in embracing my good friends like a child," he wrote at a later time to Frau von Genzinger, " only I lament that the great

Mozart will not be among them, if it be true, which I hope not, that he is dead. Posterity will not find such talent again for a century." He was the one who was destined to be the heir of Mozart, and it was his London visit which broadened his intellectual horizon and gave his fancy freer development. He was then the direct guide of Beethoven, whose sonatas, quartets and symphonies were more closely developed and patterned upon the works which Haydn had then written than upon Mozart's, the marvelous beauty of whose music was more like an inspiration from above, which could scarcely be appropriated or imitated by his followers.

His letters to Frau von Genzinger abound in information about the events of this journey, and, thanks to the detailed investigation of C. F. Pohl in his little book, " Mozart and Haydn in London " (Vienna: 1867), we are now placed in full possession of them, but we shall confine ourselves only to those details which are indispensable to a record of Haydn's progress.

In Munich, Haydn became acquainted with Cannabich, who had so greatly promoted symphony performances in Germany—an acquaintance which must have been of two-fold interest to the founder of the symphony. In Bonn, particularly, where his music had many friends, and had been played exceedingly often in churches, theaters, public and chamber-concerts (see Beethoven's Life, Vol. I), he was astonished on one occasion, according to Dies' narrative. Salomon took him on Christmas night to the mass. "The first chords revealed a work of Haydn's. Our Haydn regarded it as an accident, though it was very agreeable to him to listen to one of his own works," it is said. Towards the close, a person approached him and invited him to enter the oratory. Haydn was not a little astonished when he saw that the Elector Maximilian had summoned him. He took him by the hand and addressed his musicians in these words: " Let me make you acquainted with your highly cherished Haydn." The Elector allowed him time for them to become acquainted, and then invited him to his table. The invitation caused him a little embarrassment, for he and Salomon had arranged a little dinner in their own house. Haydn took refuge in excuses,

8

and thereupon withdrew and betook himself
to his residence, where he was surprised by an
unexpected proof of the good will of the Elect-
or.   At his quiet command, the little dinner
had changed into a large one for twelve persons, and the most skillful of the musicians had
been invited.   Could the Elector's court organist, Beethoven, have been among the guests?
He was at that time twenty years old, and certainly was among the most skillful of the musicians.

Haydn writes about the remainder of the
journey and his arrival in London, to his friend
in Vienna.   He remained on deck during the
entire passage, that he might observe to his
heart's content that huge monster, the sea.
He might have thought with an ironical smile
of the storm in "The Devil on Two Sticks."
He was completely overwhelmed " with the
endlessly great city of London, which aston-
ishes me with its varied beauties and wonders,"
but it still further broadened his experience
to see with his own eyes the representatives of
a great free people like those of England.   His
arrival had already caused a great sensation,
and for three days he went the rounds of all

the newspapers. After a few days he was in- vited to an amateur concert, and leaning upon the arm of the director, passed through the hall to the front of the orchestra amid univer- sal applause, "stared at by all and greeted with a multitude of English compliments." After- ward he was conducted to a table set for two hundred guests, where he was requested to sit at the head, but he declined the honor, since he had already dined out, that noon, and eaten more than usual; but in spite of this he was obliged to drink the harmonious good health of the company in Burgundy.

This brilliancy of welcome characterized Haydn's London visit until its close. Both so- cially and as an artist he knew how to win hearts to himself. His countryman, Gyrowetz, introduced him to fashionable families which gave entertainments, where Haydn was the cen- ter of attraction. His simple and cordial man- ner and its great contrast with the imperious manner which the Italian artists assumed upon the strength of their long residence, suited the English, and when he rose from the table, seated himself at the piano and sang the cheerful German songs, all, even the most

prejudiced, circulated his fame.   Instances
like that of the insulting slur of the once so
celebrated, but at that time old and conceited,
Italian violinist, Giardini, who received the
announcement of his visit with the remark,
"there is nothing for me to learn from the
German dog," were rare, but Haydn instead
of being angry only laughed at his folly.   In
contrast with such arrogance, he cherished
genuine artists, as we know from his association
with the great organ-player, Dupuis.   Sir G.
Smart, so well known to us from "Beethoven's
Life," relates that he saw him listening with
close attention to Dupuis' playing at St. James
church, and that when the latter came out of
the chapel, Haydn embraced and kissed him.
The unanimous recognition of others' merits
was a natural characteristic of Haydn as well
as of Mozart.   The newspapers had something
to say about him every day, but already that
envy and malice began, against which he, like
every other one of prominence, had had to
contend from youth up.   They discovered that
his powers were in their decadence, and on that
account it was useless to longer expect anything like his earlier productions.   And

this, too, when the Salomon concerts had commenced and achieved the highest success, since every new work of the master brought him new fame. The Professional Concerts, under the direction of the violinist Cramer, who had offered him an engagement in 1787, were his worst enemies. It was the professors, or the professional musicians, who arranged these, and society rivalry led them to look upon his success with an envious eye. And yet Haydn was present at their first concert of the season which preceded the Salomon concerts, and had complimented them upon performing his symphonies so well without having had the opportunity of hearing them.

Salomon's first concert met with decided success. It was of special advantage that Haydn in his judicious way knew how to secure a particular freedom of performance from his orchestra. He would flatter his players and delicately mingle blame and praise. He invited the best among them to dine, and besides all this, he took pains to practically explain his ideas to them, so that the result, as Dies emphatically says, was affection and inspiration. He would induce the Italian singers themselves, who sedulously avoided every difficulty and discord, to execute his frequently surprising modulations and intonations. " Never, perhaps, have we had richer musical enjoyment," says the *Morning Chronicle,* speaking of the concert, "and the Adagio of his symphony in D was encored —a very rare occurrence." His opera " Orpheus and Eurydice " for Gallini's new theater, though nearly completed, was not performed, as the opening of the stage was not allowed. It has numbers of equal merit with the best that Haydn has written, but as a whole it is modeled upon the usual Italian pattern of separate airs. Haydn's genius revealed itself otherwise in his own special sphere, and except the quartets, the most of his instrumental music which has come down to us had its origin at this time in London, especially the twelve London symphonies. They display in the clearest manner the increased development of his ideas and fancy, the deepening of his thought and the rich and firm handling of instruments which place Haydn on the same plane as Mozart and Beethoven. He had an orchestra which in strength and skill was second to none in the world at that time; at the same time, the efforts to produce artistic impressions, which seize upon the mind and heart, aroused and invigorated his large and sympathetic, if not always really musical, audiences. It was Haydn who first created the love of pure instrumental music in the heart of the great public of London, where vocal music since Handel's time had been more highly valued than elsewhere, and this, too, not alone for its earnest, but for its humorous moods, which were more readily appreciated by Englishmen. It was, however, his quartets which were sought by the real friends and students of music, and the best of these also were written in and for London.

At the end of May, Haydn attended the great Handel Festival, which had been given every year since 1784, and in which over one thousand musicians took part. Even the sight of the great assemblage was brilliant and magnificent, but beyond all this, he had the opportunity of hearing Handel's music in its full majesty. More than twenty of his large and minor works were performed, and the powerful personal influence of the master dominated the performance. When the world-renowned " Hallelujah " rose in great waves of sound, and the thousands, with the king at their head, stood up, there was scarcely a dry eye. Haydn, who stood near the king's box, wept like a child, and completely overcome, exclaimed: " He is the master of us all." The sublimity of the all-overmastering Eternal he never displays in his own works. He was, so to speak, forced out of the church into life, and never found his way back again to its sublime earnestness, but the religious feeling and simple piety of the heart were active, living principles in Haydn's nature, and gave to his forms that breath of living creation which transforms them into the "divine likeness." The perfect innocence and the touching and beautiful earnestness which often appear in his works, come from the same source as Handel's majesty sublimity. His " Creation " is a still more convincing illustration of this. Its origin was due to the London visit, and many a large and important choral piece bears witness to the fact that Haydn had now met and seen this Handel face to face. He was to him what Sebastian Bach was to Mozart and Bee-

thoven, whom he had not known so well as
they. On the 8th of July, 1791, after his
brilliant season had come to a close, Haydn received a special mark of distinction. The degree of Doctor of Music was conferred upon
him by the University of Oxford. At the last
festival concert, when he entered, clad in his
black silk doctor's gown and four-cornered
cap, he was enthusiastically received. He
seized the skirt of his gown, and held it up
with a loud "I thank you," which simple expression of gratitude was greeted with universal applause. This respect for England served
to make him still more famous. Salomon was
warranted in announcing, a month later, that
they would continue their concerts in the same
style as those which had made such a success
in the winter.

Meanwhile, an entirely unexpected sum-
mons to return to Esterhaz reached him. He
was expected to write the opera for a festivity
at the Prince's court. Evidently he could not
comply, for he had signed new terms of agreement with Salomon, and thus had to encounter
the Prince's anger for his desertion of duty.

" Alas, I now expect my discharge, but I

hope that God will be gracious and help me in some measure to efface my losses by my industry," he wrote to Frau von Genzinger, September 17, 1791, and this industry was made less burdensome as he had spent the summer in the country, amid beautiful scenery, with a family whose hearts, he writes, resemble the Genzingers. How much must he, who was so accustomed to Nature, have appreciated such a country visit! "I am, God be thanked, in good health, with the exception of my customary rheumatism. I am working industriously, and think every morning, as I walk alone in the woods with my English grammar, of my Creator, of my family, and of all the friends I have left behind," he writes in his seclusion, which, as we see, brought him the most beautiful outward and inward happiness. Added to this was his consciousness of being free. "O, my dear gracious lady, what a sweet relish there is in absolute liberty," he writes again; "I have it now in some degree; I appreciate its benefits, although my mind is burdened with more work. The consciousness that I am no longer a servant requites all my toil." He realized there also a striking confirmation of the happiness of rising "from nothing." His landlord, a rich banker, was so impressed with his narrative of his youthful trials, that he once swore that he was getting on too well in the world. He realized for the first time that he was not happy. "I have only an abundance and I loathe it," he exclaimed, and wished he had a pistol that he might shoot himself, an event, however, which did not happen, much to Haydn's pleasure.

After his return to London he encountered exciting times, for the Professional musicians bent all their energies to surpass the Salomon concerts, and their public assaults had such an extended influence that inquiries came from Vienna about the actual condition of his circumstances. Even Mozart believed these reports and thought he must have depreciated very much. "I can not believe it," Haydn simply writes, and refers him to his banker, Count Fries, in whose hands he had placed five hundred pounds. "I am aware that there is a multitude of envious persons in London, the most of whom are Italians, but they can not hurt me, for my credit with the people has been settled many years," he says, and adds with confident feeling: "Those above them are my support."

As their next move, the Professionals sought to secure him for themselves by higher offers, but he would not break his word or injure his manager, whose outlay had been so large, by the gratification of sordid motives. So they renewed their assaults upon his age and the pretended decadence of his ability, and announced that they had secured his pupil Pleyel. The latter, a neighbor and countryman of Haydn, was at that time thirty-four years of age and twenty-five years the younger. Mozart had expressed a favorable opinion of his talent. He writes to his father in 1784 about Pleyel's new quartets: "If you do not yet know them, try to get them; it is worth the trouble. You will at once recognize his master. It will be a good and fortunate thing for music if Pleyel in his day is able to supply Haydn's place for us." He was unquestionably innocent in the matter of the invitation to come to London, and really made his appearance in the season of 1792.

Meanwhile, Haydn had spent two days with

the Duke of York, who had married the seven-teen-year-old Princess Ulrica, of Prussia, daughter of King Frederick William II. In 1787, her music-loving father had sent him a ring, which he wore as a talisman, and a very complimentary letter, for six new quartets. "She is the most charming lady in the world, is very intelligent, plays the piano and sings very agreeably," writes Haydn. "The dear little lady sat near me and hummed all the pieces, which she knew by heart, having heard them so often in Berlin. The Duke's broth-er, the Prince of Wales, played the 'cello ac-companiment very acceptably. He loves mu-sic exceedingly, has very much feeling but very little money. His goodness, however, pleases me more than any self-interest," he says in conclusion. The Prince also had Haydn's portrait painted for his cabinet.

Many more personal attentions of a similar kind were paid him. One Mr. Shaw made a silver lid for a snuff-box which Haydn had given him, and inscribed thereon, " Presented by the renowned Haydn." His very beauti-ful wife—" the mistress is the most beautiful woman I have ever seen," he writes in his diary—embroidered his name in gold upon a ribbon which he preserved even when a very old man. It was at this time he received with bitter tears the news of Mozart's death. "Mozart died December 5, 1791," he simply writes in his diary, but we know the beautiful remark he made to his friend in Vienna who had so often played Mozart's masterpieces for him. At a later period he said in a similar strain to Griesinger: "Mozart's loss is irretrievable. I can never forget his playing in my life. It went to the heart." In the year 1807, speaking to other musical friends in Vienna, he said with tears in his eyes: "Pardon me, I must always weep at the name of my Mozart." Indeed, at this time he must have deeply felt the contrast between the brilliancy of this genius and the darkness of his own outer life in these declining years. And yet he felt all the more the importance of preserving the respect for German art. In the midst of such times as these Pleyel arrived. "So there will now be a bloody harmonious war between master and scholar," he writes, but on the other hand they were frequently together. "Pleyel displayed so much

modesty upon his arrival that he won my
love anew. We are very often together,
which is to his credit, and he knows how to
prize his father. We will share our fame
alike, and each one will go home contented,"
he says. He too must have longed for his
Austrian home, or he would have acted differently towards " Papa."

One of the newspapers rightly understood
the situation. " Haydn and Pleyel are offset
against each other this season, and both
parties are earnest rivals, yet as both belong
to the same rank as composers, they will not
share the petty sentiments of their respective
admirers," says the *Public Advertiser*, and so
it eventuated, though not until after many
painful experiences for both the men, for
with the others' plans there was mingled very
much of personal animosity. The Professionals announced twelve new compositions of
Pleyel's. Early in 1792 Haydn writes to
Vienna : " In order to keep my word and
support poor Salomon, I must be the victim,
and work incessantly. I really feel it. My
eyes suffer the most. My mind is very weary,
and it is only the help of God that will sup-

ply what is wanting in my power. I daily pray to Him, for without His assistance I am but a poor creature." The best hours of the day he was compelled to devote to visits and private musicals. "I have never written in any one year of my life as much as in the last," he says, and yet his works show all the charming freshness of youth, with the contrast of greater depth and richer illustration. He found time to arrange twelve Scotch songs, and he says, "I am proud of this work, and flatter myself that it will live many years after I am gone." But they made a complete failure, and the publishers therefore made a subsequent application to Beethoven.

The professional concerts at this time again had the precedence, and it is a fair illustration of their rivalry, that at the commencement they brought out a symphony of his and sent him a personal invitation. "They criticise Pleyel's presumption very much, but I admire him none the less. I have been to all his concerts, and was the first to applaud him," he writes to Vienna. In his first concert he also brought out a symphony of Pleyel's. His own new symphony, notwithstanding he thought the last movement was weak, made "the deepest impression upon his audience." The Adagio had to be repeated, and the entire work was performed again in the eighth and eighteenth concerts, by " request." For the second concert he wrote a chorus, " The Storm." It was the first which he had composed with English text, and it met with extraordinary success, because in it were united the most striking qualities of his art, skill, and good humor. As he himself writes, he gained considerable credit with the English in vocal music and this was destined to have a decisive result.

At the sixth concert, March 23, 1792, the symphony with the kettle-drum effect was given. Haydn says of it : " It was a convenient opportunity for me to surprise the public with something new. The first Allegro was received with innumerable bravas, but the Andante aroused the enthusiasm to the highest pitch. 'Encore, encore,' resounded on every side, and Pleyel himself complimented me upon my effects." Gyrowetz visited him after its completion to hear it upon the piano. At the drum-passage, Haydn, certain of its success,

9

with a roguish laugh, exclaimed: "There the women will jump." Dies gives the current version of the original cause of the work as follows: The ladies and gentlemen in the concerts, which took place after the late English dinners, often indulged in a nap, and Haydn thought he would waken them in this comic manner. The English call the symphony, "The Surprise," and among all the twelve, it is to this day, the favorite.

How deeply Haydn's music impressed his English hearers, and how clearly it appears that they for the first time recognized the soul of music, disclosing to the popular mind its mysterious connection with the Infinite, is evident from a strange entry in Haydn's diary. A clergyman, upon hearing the Andante of one of his symphonies, sank into the deepest melancholy, because he had dreamed the night before its performance, that the piece announced his death. He immediately left the assemblage, and took to his bed. "I heard to-day, April 25, that this clergyman died," writes Haydn. It is the elementary revelations of the deepest feeling and individual spiritual certitude that speak to us in Haydn's music, and they have, so to speak, the most powerful grasp upon our individual existence. Indeed, they explain the irresistible and immeasurable influence of music. It is the image of Infinity itself, while the other arts are only the images of its phenomena. Its influence is so much more powerful and impressive than that of the other arts, because, as the philosopher would say, they represent only the shadow of things, while music represents their actual existence. A people so pre-eminently metaphysical and serious in character as the English, must have taken this simple, but deeply thoughtful Haydn and his symphonies into their very hearts. How could they have awarded the palm to any one living at that time over him? He had himself thoroughly comprehended the deep-lying genius of this nation, and in the province of *his* genius he could lead it to a point its own nature could not reach. Every one of his compositions written for London, as well as those subsequently, show this, and many of his utterances illustrate his esteem for the English public. " The score was much more acceptable to me because much of it I had to change to suit the English taste," he writes in March, 1792, when his long wished for symphony in E major had been forwarded to him from Vienna. And it should be remembered among all these events that Handel had written all his oratorios in and for London, and Beethoven's Ninth was " the symphony for London."

In May, 1792, Haydn had a benefit concert, at which two new symphonies were performed, and this, like the last concert, met with such favor, that Salomon offered the public an extra concert with the works that had been most admired during the season. "Salomon closed his season with the greatest eclat," says the *Morning Herald*, and Pohl simply and appropriately adds : " Haydn was in all his glory, beloved, admired and courted. His name was the main stay of every concert-giver. Painters and engravers immortalized their art by his picture." One such, a highly characteristic profile portrait, by George Dance, is given with the English edition (1867) of the "Musical Letters." * It confirms the description of

---

* [This portrait, copied from the original, will be found in the frontispiece of this volume.—TRANSLATOR.]

his appearance, which has already been given, in every feature.

Before his departure, he had another experience, which clearly indicates and reveals the source of music in his nature. At the yearly gathering of the Charity Scholars at St. Paul's cathedral, he heard four thousand children sing a simple hymn. "I was more touched by this devout and innocent music than by any I ever heard in my life," he says in his diary, and he adds in confirmation of it: "I stood and wept like a child."

With this impression were unconsciously associated the most active memories of his own home, from which he had been absent so long. The home-image never rises so vividly in our hearts as when we see these little ones who are so particularly the active genii of the house and home. He stated, as the principal reason for his return, his wish to enjoy the pleasure of his fatherland; and he wrote in December, 1791, that he could not reconcile himself to spend his life in London, even if he could amass millions. Other artists have also borne testimony to the influence of the Festival alluded to above. In 1837, Berlioz attended it with the violinist Duprez and John Cramer. "Never have I seen Duprez in such a state; he stammered, wept, and raved," says Berlioz. The latter, in order to get a better view of the whole scene, donned a surplice, and placed himself among the accompanying basses, where, more than once, "like Agamemnon with his toga," he covered his face with his music sheets, overcome with the sight of the children and the sound of their voices. As they were going out, Duprez exclaimed in delight, speaking in Italian instead of French, in his excitement: "Marvelous! marvelous! The glory of England!"

Haydn might well have thought the same, for he had already made a deep impression upon the nation, and touched its heart with the kindly feelings of life.

It was his last great experience "in the vast city of London," and to Haydn's inner nature it gave in brief all that he had given and all that was due to him. It was the first time he had seen a vast multitude of human beings in a great and eagerly listening throng, and it expanded his own nature, which had been restricted, to the widest bounds, without in any

way modifying its power.   He had experienced the full measure of English humor, manifesting itself in those relations of personal
affection which the " beautiful and gracious "
Mrs. Schroter had expressed for him and his
" sweet " compositions—an affection which she
herself regarded as " one of the greatest blessings of her life," and which had bound her to
him in an indissoluble attachment.   " My
heart was, and still is, full of tenderness for
you, yet words can not express half the love
and affection which I feel for you.   You are
dearer to me every day of my life," she says at
another time.   That it was the deep principle
and character of his life which had aroused
such a passionate affection in the already aged
lady, these words confess : " Truly, dearest, no
tongue can express the gratitude which I feel
for the unbounded delight your music has
given me."   The fact that this loving esteem
was meant for Haydn himself, makes it all the
more beautiful.

Such were the satisfying and grateful feelings which filled his soul at the moment of
parting.   Outwardly and inwardly blessed, he
returned to Vienna in July, 1792, and not
two years later, he was again on the Thames.

CHAPTER IV.

THE EMPEROR'S HYMN—THE CREATION AND THE SEASONS.

1793—1809.

ON his journey back, in July, 1792, Haydn again visited Bonn. The court musicians gave him a breakfast at the suburb of Godesburg, and Beethoven laid before him a cantata, probably the one written on the death of Leopold II, to which the master gave special attention and "encouraged its author to assiduous study." The arrangements were unquestionably made at that time, by which the young composer afterward became Haydn's scholar, "for Beethoven even then had surprised every one with his remarkable piano playing."

(136)

Since the death of Gluck and Mozart, Haydn had been recognized in Vienna, and indeed in all Germany, as the first master. In the spring of 1792 the *Musikalische Correspondenz* declared that his services were so universally recognized, and the influence of his numerous works was so effective, that his style appeared to be the sole aim of composers, and they approached more closely to perfection the nearer they approached him. The fame he had won in England was no longer doubted or disputed. Every account spoke of him in a manner that betrayed a feeling of national pride, says Dies, and all the more was this the case after he had brought out his six new symphonies in the Burg Theater, on the 22nd and 23rd of December, to which very naturally, eager attention was given in Vienna. His success was of great advantage to that same Tonkunstler Societat which had once treated him so shabbily. He was elected a member, exempt from dues, but it was never necessary to make any claim upon him.

The " country of wealth " had so materially improved his fortune that he bought a little house in a " retired, quiet place " in the sub-

urb of Gumpendorf, which his wife, with the
utmost naivete, had picked out for herself,
when she should become a widow, but which
became his own resting-place in his old age.
He added a story to it afterward and lived
there until his death, surviving his wife about
nine years.

Composition and instruction still remained
his regular quiet work. The lessons at this
time, in the case of one scholar at least, were
pretty troublesome. "Haydn has announced
that he shall give up large works to him, and
must soon cease composing," one writes from
Bonn, at the beginning of 1793, referring to
Beethoven. It was a characteristic of the old
master that he advised the young scholar,
three of whose trios (op. 1) had been played
before him and about which he had said
many complimentary things, not to publish
the third, in C minor. He feared that the rest
of the music, in contrast with such "storm
and stress," would appear tame and spiritless,
and that it would rather hurt than help him
in the estimation of the public. This made a
bad impression upon the easily suspicious
Beethoven. He believed Haydn was envious

and jealous and meant no good to him. Thus it appears, that from the very beginning *all* confidence in the instruction was destroyed, and, besides this, it had little prospect of success, since the still more revolutionary youth had gone far beyond his fame-crowned senior in his innovations. Still he remained until the end of the year 1793, and the greater youth never forgot what he owed the great master. " Coffee for Haydn and myself," and other observations of a like character in Beethoven's diary, show, that besides the matter of instruction there was a personal friendly intercourse between them. Ostensibly it discontinued when Haydn's second journey offered a fitting pretext, but, as a matter of fact, he was at that time a scholar of Schenk, who is mentioned in Mozart's biography. He had very often complained to other musicians that he did not get on well with his studies, since Haydn was occupied altogether too much with his work and could not devote the requisite attention to him. Schenk, who had already heard Beethoven extemporize at one of his associates,' the abbe Gelinek, met him one day, as he was returning from Haydn, with his music under his arm, glanced it over and found that several errors remained uncorrected. This decided Beethoven's change and choice.

Notwithstanding all this, it was reported in Bonn from Vienna, in the summer of 1793, that the young countryman made great progress in art, and this was to Haydn's credit, who, with the help of his Fux and Philip Emanuel Bach, was able to collect and arrange the well acquired theoretical knowledge of the "genial stormer," in a practical manner, and thereby substantially raised him to his own rank, although he did not comply with the understood wish of his teacher that he would place " Scholar of Haydn" upon the sonatas (op. 2), dedicated to him, because, as he declared in justification of his refusal, that he had not learned anything from him. This remark refers to the higher instruction in composition, where their ideas differed. Yet in 1793, he went with Haydn to Eisenstadt, and he had even intended to go with him the next winter to England. Beethoven's pupil, Ries, also expressly says that Haydn highly esteemed Beethoven, but as he was so stubborn and self-willed, he called him " the great Mogul."

How entirely free from envy Haydn was towards younger artists at this time, is shown by a note to his godson, Joseph Weigl, afterward the composer of the "Schweizer Familie." "It is long since I have felt such enthusiasm for any music as yesterday in hearing your 'Princess of Amalfi,'" he writes to him, January 11, 1794. "It is full of good ideas, sublime, expressive, in short, a master piece; I felt the warmest interest in the well deserved applause that greeted it. Keep a place for an old boy like me in your memory." He had always helped to open the way for the young scholar into the best musical circles of Vienna, and now that the teacher was again about to depart, the scholar could seek his own fortune without going astray.

The preparation of the necessary works for this second journey had been the too constant occupation of the old man. It must have been undertaken however for other reasons than these; for Haydn knew that he must have something to live upon, even in his simple manner, in his unemployed old age. It was not right that a self-willed young beginner, who paid nothing for his instruction, as he had

no other means of support except his salary
from the Elector, should take up too much of
his valuable time. It was enough to impart
the main points of instruction without giving
any attention to little and merely incidental
errors which would disappear of themselves in
time. We know Haydn's views of such things,
and there was a characteristic illustration of
them in his later days. The contrapuntist, Albrechtsberger, Beethoven's subsequent teacher, who, according to the latter's witty statement, at best only created musical skeletons
with his art, insisted that consecutive fourths
should be banished from strict composition.
"What is the good of that?" said Haydn.
"Art is free and should not be tied down with
mechanical rules. Such artifices are of no value.
I would prefer instead that some one would
try to compose a new minuet." Beethoven
actually did this, and called it, in his op. 1,
Scherzo. "Haydn rarely escaped without a
side cut," says Ries of Beethoven—but however all this may be, we may not only imagine
but we know that this opposition between
the two artists, which arose from their different temperaments, made no real difference in
Beethoven's respect for Haydn.

We now come to the second London journey. This time the Prince interposed objections. He desired indeed no personal service, but he had a pride in Haydn and his fame, and thought he had secured sufficient glory. He may also have thought that a man sixty years old ought not to expose himself to the hardships of a distant journey, and the persecutions of envy. Haydn appreciated his good intentions, but he still felt strong, and preferred an active life to the quiet in which his Prince had placed him. Besides, he knew that the English public would still recognize his genius, and he had engaged with Salomon to write six more symphonies, and had many profitable contracts with various publishers in London. The Prince at last gave way and allowed Haydn to go, never to see him again, for he died shortly afterward, and Haydn had the fourth of the Esterhazys for patron and master, upon whose order he composed a requiem while in London as a tribute to the departed.

On the 19th of January, 1794, the journey began. While at Scharding, an incident happened which clearly shows Haydn's good hu

mor.   The customs officers asked what his
occupation was.   Haydn informed them, " A
tone-artist;" (Tonkunstler), "What is that?"
they replied. " Oh ! yes, a potter, (Thonkunst-
ler), said one.   "That's it," averred Haydn,
" and this one," (his faithful servant, Elssler)
" is my partner."   At Wiesbaden, he realized
with much satisfaction the greatness of his
fame.   At the inn his Andante with the kettle-
drum effect, which had so quickly become a favorite, was played in a room near by him.
Dies says: "He regarded the player as his
friend, and courteously entered the room.   He
found some Prussian officers, all of whom were
great admirers of his works, and when he at
last disclosed himself they would not believe
he was Haydn.   ' Impossible ! impossible !
you, Haydn ! a man already so old ! this does
not agree with the fire in your music.'   The
gentlemen continued so long in this strain that
at last he exhibited the letter received from
his king, which he always carried in his chest
for good luck.   Thereupon the officers overwhelmed him with their attentions, and he
was compelled to remain in their company
until long after midnight."

This time Haydn lived very near to his friend and admirer, Frau Schroter, yet we learn nothing further of their relations to each other. The leading accounts of this second visit have not been kept, but in reality they repeat the events of the first. His name this time was free from detraction. They agreed that his power had increased, and that one of the new symphonies was his best work. His name was in request for every concert-programme, and the repetition of his pieces was as frequent as during his first visit. "In geniality and talent who is like him?" says the *Oracle*, March 10, 1794.

Sir G. Smart in 1866, then in his ninetieth year, and who was a violin player with Salomon, relates a neat story of this time, to Pohl, the biographer. At a rehearsal there was need of a drummer. Haydn asked: "Is there any one here who can play the kettle-drum?" "I can," quickly replied young Smart, who never had had a drum stick in his hand, but thought that correct time was all that was necessary. After the first movement, Haydn went to him and praised him, but intimated to him that in Germany they required

10

strokes which would not stop the vibrations of
the drum. At the same time he took the
sticks and exhibited to the astonished orchestra an entirely new style of drumming.
"Very well," replied the undaunted young
Smart, "if you prefer to have this style, we
can do it just as well in England." Haydn's
first drum lessons with his cousin Frankh, in
Hamburg, will readily occur to the reader.

On the 12th of May, 1794, the Military
Symphony, another favorite among all Haydn's friends, was performed for the first time.
It overflows with genial merriment, and often
with genuine frolicsome humor. Not long
afterward, the news reached him that the new
Prince Nicholas wished to reorganize the orchestra at Eisenstadt, and had appointed him
anew as Capellmeister. Haydn received this
news with great pleasure. This princely house
had assured him a living, and, what was of
still more importance, had given him the opportunity of fully developing his talent as
a composer. His profits in London far ex-
ceeded his salary in the Fatherland, and a
persistent effort was made to keep him in England, but he decided as soon as his existing

engagements were concluded to return to his old position.

A secret but very powerfully operating reason may also have been the same which to-day actuates that greatest of natural tone artists, Franz Liszt—wherever he may go, he always returns to Germany. It is the spirit of music itself which permeates every fiber of our life, in the earnest feeling of which we bathe and find health. Notwithstanding the attractive performance of the orchestra and of the virtuosi, the most of whom were Germans, the master did not find London and England peculiarly musical. What he thought of the theater is recorded in his diary: "What miserable stuff at Saddler's Wells! A fellow screamed an aria so frightfully and with such ridiculous grimaces that I began to sweat all over. N. B. He had to repeat the aria! *O uha bestie!*" There yet remained much of the English jockey style in these musico-theatrical performances, and the value of music was reckoned upon another standard than that which belongs to intellectual things. Thus we may readily believe, though Haydn himself pretended not to hear it, that the rough mob in the gallery, hissing and whistling, cried out, "Fiddler, Fiddler," when the orchestra rose to honor him, an artist and a foreigner, upon his first appearance in the theater. After these not very agreeable experiences of English musical taste, Haydn looked upon it as a comical proof of his reputation, when, as Griesinger relates, Englishmen would approach him, measure him from head to foot, and leave him with the exclamation, "You are a great man."

Still another circumstance shows how absolutely he preferred his Austrian home. In August, 1794, he visited the ruins of the old abbey of Waverly. "I must confess," he writes in his diary, that every time I look upon this beautiful ruin, my heart is troubled as I think that all this once occurred among those of my religion." His continual abode among people of the Protestant confession, so opposed to his own Catholicism, disturbed those feelings and ideas of the simple man in these later years which had swayed his inner nature for two generations. This is a matter of personal feeling, and does not affect that toleration which in all religious matters characterized his beautiful nature. Finally, political freedom, which had made England so powerful, was not agreeable to his primitive manner of life. While he says not a word of the excellencies of the life of a great free people, he several times alludes to the rude noises and frantic shouts of the "sweet mob" (suessen Poebels) in London festivals and at the theaters. Socially considered, notwithstanding the political freedom, the barriers that separated classes were just as distinct and insurmountable as they are to-day. Nowhere in the world, indeed, is custom more formal—reason enough in itself to make him love his Fatherland all the more fervently.

His fame in England, however, continually increased. He was already called a genius inferior to no one, and this, too, in the same connection with the mention of a performance of Hamlet, which he had attended. His sportive humor allied him very closely to the great English tragic poet: if not so deep and so quickly moving to tears, he still derived his power doubtless from the same simple source of feeling. He himself mentions one instance of his roguish humor while in London, according to Dies and others. He was intimately acquainted with a German who had acquired boundless dexterity in the violin technique, and was addicted to the common practice of always making effects in the extremely high tones. Haydn wished to see if he could not disgust him with this dilettantist weakness and induce a feeling for legitimate playing. The violinist often visited one Miss Janson, who played the piano very skillfully, and was accustomed to accompany him. Haydn wrote a sonata for them, called it "Jacob's Dream," and sent it anonymously to the lady, who did not hesitate to perform it with the violinist, as it appeared to be an easy little work. At first it flowed easily through passages which were begun in the third position of the violin. The violinist was in ecstasies. "Very well written. One can see the composer knows the instrument," he murmured. But in the close, instead of lowering to a practical place, it mounted to the fifth, sixth, and at last to the seventh position. His fingers continually crowded against and through each other like ants. Crawling around the instrument and stumbling over the passages, he ex-

claimed with the sweat of misery on his brow :
" Who ever heard of such scribbling ? The
man knows nothing about writing for the
violin." The lady soon discovered that the
composer meant to illustrate by these high
passages the heavenly ladder which Jacob saw
in his dream, and the more she observed her
companion stumbling around unsteadily upon
this ladder, reeling and jumping up and down,
the thing was so comical that she could not
conceal her laughter, which at length broke
out in a storm, from which we may fancy that
it cured the dilettante of his foolish passion. It
was not discovered until five or six months
afterward who the composer was, and Miss
Janson sent him a gift.

Haydn's influence upon the public during
his second visit to London is observed even in
still higher degree. Salomon, indeed, said,
though somewhat figuratively, yet openly, to
" proud England," that these Haydn concerts
were not without their influence upon the
public interests, since they had created a permanent taste for music. In the spring of 1795,
Haydn saw the royal pair several times. The
first time it was at the house of the young and

musical Duchess of York, whom the Prince of Wales had introduced to him. The Hanoverian George III, was already prepossessed in Handel's favor. Philip Emanuel Bach writes of him in 1786: "The funniest of all is the gracious precautions that are taken to preserve Handel's youthful works with the utmost care." But on this evening, when only Haydn's works were played by the royal orchestra, under Salomon's direction, and of course, excellently, he showed great interest in them also. "Dr. Haydn," said he, "you have written much." "Yes, Sire, more than is good." "Certainly not; the world disputes that." The King then presented him to the Queen, and said he knew that Haydn had once been a good singer and he would like to hear some of his songs." "Your Majesty, my voice is now only so large," said Haydn, pointing to the joint of his little finger. The King smiled, and Haydn sang his song, "Ich bin der Verliebteste." Two days afterward, there was a similar entertainment at the residence of the Prince of Wales, who required his presence very often.

He related to Griesinger that upon that occasion he directed twenty-six musicians, and the orchestra often had to wait several hours until the Prince rose from the table. As there was no compensation for all this trouble, when Parliament settled up the bills of the Prince, he sent in an account of one hundred guineas, which was promptly paid. Haydn was not very well pleased about the matter, although upon the occasion of his first acquaintance in 1791, he had written that the Prince loved music exceedingly, had very much feeling, but very little money, and that he desired his good will more than any self-interest. Still he had, as his will shows, many poor relatives, who had claims upon him, and was it right that he should lose at the hands of the princely son of the richest land in the world, upon whom he had bestowed such faithful artistic services? While yet in London he met with a bitter proof of what he was to endure on account of these relatives. He was compelled to immediately settle the debt of a married nephew, who was the major-domo of the Esterhazy family, and we see by his will that these relatives had squandered more than six thousand florins of his through his great kindness. His remarkable goodness was as much an obligation in his estimation, as nobility or genius in others, and he never allowed any possible means of practicing it to escape without some good cause.

He was repeatedly invited to the Queen's concerts, and was also presented by her with the manuscript of Handel's "Savior at the Cross." As Germans, both she and the King were eager to keep him in England. " I will give you a residence at Windsor for the summer," said the Queen, "and then " with a roguish glance at the King, "we can some times have tete-a-tete music." " O, I am not jealous of Haydn," said the King, "he is a good and noble German." "To maintain that reputation is my highest ambition," quickly exclaimed Haydn. After repeated efforts to persuade him, he replied that he was bound by gratitude to the house of his Prince, and that he could not always remain away from his fatherland and his wife. The King begged him to let the latter come. "She never crosses the Danube, still less the sea," replied Haydn. He remained inflexible on this point, and he believed that it was on this account that he received no gift from the

King, and that no further interest was manifested in him by the court. The real and deeper reason for his decision we have already learned.

The concerts of the year 1795 were laid out upon a more magnificent scale than before, as political events upon the continent had disturbed the interest in them in various ways. Haydn, Martini, Clementi, and the most distinguished players and singers from all countries—London had never witnessed more brilliant concert-schemes. Haydn opened the second part of every concert with a symphony. The *Oracle* says of one of these: "It shows the fancy and style of Haydn in forms that are not at the command of any other genius." After he gave his benefit concert, May 4, 1795, upon which occasion the Military Symphony and the Symphony in D major, the last of the twelve London series, were played, he wrote in his diary: "The hall was filled with a select company. They were extremely pleased and so was I. I made this evening four thousand florins. It is only in England one can make so much." These pleasant experiences gave him the idea of writing a work of the

style which was very popular and greatly esteemed in England—the oratorio.   He had
begun one such with English text, which was
unfinished, however, because he could not express himself with sufficient feeling in that
language.

He was the recipient of many gifts at this
time, among them a cocoanut cup with a silver standard from Clementi; a silver dish, a
foot in width, from the well known Tattersall,
for his help in the work of improving the
English church music; and even nine years
later, the influences of his London visit were
apparent in a gift sent to him of six pairs of
woolen stockings, upon which were embroidered six themes of his music, like the Andante
from the drum symphony, the "Emperor's
Hymn," etc.   He was the first, since Handel's
time, who had universally and permanently
succeeded with his music in London, and
had impressed his listeners with an earnest
and realizing sense of the real meaning of
music.   He was the first, for when Mozart,
and afterward Beethoven, were known in
London, a new dynasty began.   Now Haydn
ruled as firmly as Handel had previously.

He had established his pre-eminence by the immense number of works of all kinds he had written. Griesinger gives a list in his own catalogue comprising in all seven hundred and sixty-eight pages, among which, besides the opera of "Orpheus" and the twelve London symphonies, whose subjects are given in the volume, "Haydn in London," there are six quartets, eleven sonatas, and countless songs, dances and marches—indeed, there is no end to them. The work that made his sway absolute was "The Creation," the text of which had been given to him by Salomon while still in London, where he had acquired "much credit in vocal music," and the crowning close, so to speak, of his London visit was made at home.

In August, 1795, Haydn returned to Vienna by way of Hamburg and Dresden, as the French held possession of the Rhine. This time his journey had been very profitable. His second visit had added an equal amount to the twelve thousand florins made in his first, and he also retained his publisher's royalties in England as well as in Germany and Paris. He could now contemplate his old age without any apprehensions since he had a certainty to live upon, though a modest one. "Haydn often insisted that he first became famous in Germany after he had been in England,' says Griesinger. The value of his works was recognized, but that public homage, which surpassing talent usually enjoys, first came to him in old age, and for this reason now we call him "our immortal Haydn." On the 18th of December, 1795, he gave a concert again in Vienna with his new compositions, but this time for his own personal profit. Three new symphonies were played. He was overwhelmed with attentions and his receipts were more than a thousand guldens. Beethoven assisted in this concert, a proof of the good feeling existing at this time between teacher and scholar.

One day the Baron Van Swieten, who is well known in connection with the time of Beethoven and Mozart, and whom he had known for twenty years or more, said to him "We must now have an oratorio from you also, dear Haydn." "He assisted me at times with a couple of ducats and sent me also an easy traveling carriage on my second journey to England," says Haydn. The Emperor's librarian, Van Swieten, was secretary of an aristocratic society, whose associates illustrated the real meaning of that term, as they comprised the entire musical nobility of Europe— Esterhazy, Lobkowitz, Kinsky, Lichnowsky, Schwarzenberg, Auersperg, Trautmannsdorf and others. They had been accustomed for years to bring out large vocal works in the beautiful library-hall of the imperial city. Handel was the chosen favorite, and Mozart had arranged for these concerts the "Acis and Galatea," "Ode to St. Cecilia," "Alexander's Feast" and "The Messiah." They did not possess or they did not yet know anything of this style in Germany, for Sebastian Bach had not been discovered in Vienna. Haydn's "Ruckkehr des Tobias," like Mozart's "Davidde penitente," was written in a style which belonged to the opera, and the "Requiem" was already at hand and had been performed, but they were the only things of their class. On the other hand the "Zauberfloete" had drawn thousands to the theater, year in and year out. Why could they not hear this characteristic pure German music in the concert-hall? In this work there was, so to speak, a specimen of the " Creation " with animals, beings and the Paradise on every hand, in which the loving pair, Pamina and Tamino, are solemnly tested. How much more varied appear the life-pictures in Lidley's " Creation "—a poem which Haydn had placed in Van Swieten's hands! The society, without doubt upon Swieten's suggestion, guaranteed the sum of five hundred ducats and the latter made the translation of the English text. Three years later the most popular of all oratorios, " The Creation," was completed.

Meanwhile, with the exception of the Mass which was the product of the war-time of 1796, in which the Agnus Dei commence with kettle-drums as if one heard the enemy already coming in the distance, an artistic event occurred which, if not reaching the limits of musical art as such, yet in the most beautiful manner fulfilled its lofty mission of welding together the conceptions and feeling of all times and peoples, and directing them to a high mission—it was the composition of " God Save the Emperor Francis."

This song has its origin in the revolutionary

agitations of the year (1796), brought over
from France, which determined the Imperial
High Chancellor, Count Saurau, to have a
national song written which should display
" before all the world the true devotion of the
Austrian people to their good and upright
father of his country, and to arouse in the
hearts of all good Austrians that noble national pride which was essential to the energet-
tic accomplishment of all the beneficial measures of the sovereign." He then applied to
our immortal countryman, Haydn, whom he
regarded as the only one competent to write
something like the English " God Save the
King." In reality this minister aroused the
noblest German popular spirit, and established
it in a beautiful setting, far exceeding his restricted purpose at the outset. Haydn himself had already arranged the English national hymn in London. More than once,
upon the occasion of public festivals, it had
afforded him the opportunity of learning in
the most convincing manner the strong attachment of the English to their royal house,
the embodiment of their State. He had also
preserved his own devotion to his Fatherland

11

through many a sharp test. His long continued stay in a foreign land had only served to
fully convince him what his Austrian home
and Germany were to him. Above all, the
music represents not merely his own most original utterance of the people, and he, who had
already learned the Lied in the childhood of
the people itself, had been the first to introduce it in a becoming and all-joyous manner
in the art of music.

Thus his full heart was in this composition,
and the commission came to him, as it were,
direct from his Emperor. Far more than
"God Save the King," this Emperor's Hymn
is an outburst of universal popular feeling.
The "Heil dir im Siegerkranz," or any
special Fatherland-song, could not be the
German people's hymn, and the "Deutschland, Deutschland uber Alles" has only become so, because it was set to Haydn's melody,
which accounts for its speedy and universal
adoption as the people's hymn. The German
people realize in it the spirit of their own life,
in its very essence, as closely as music can express it. In reality, there is no people's hymn
richer, or, we might say, more satisfying in

feeling, than this. The "God Save the King,"
so fine in itself, of which Beethoven said he
must sometime show the English what a
blessing they had in its melody, appears poor
and thin in contrast with such fullness of mel-
odic rhythm and manifold modulation.   In
the second verse the melody produces with
most beautiful effect that mysterious exaltation
which enthralls us when in accord with the
grandest impulses of the people, and the re-
sponsive portion of the second part—the climax of the whole—carries this exalted feeling,
as it were, upon the waves of thousands and
thousands of voices to the very dome of
Eternity.   The construction of the melody is
a masterpiece of the first order.   Never has a
grander or more solid development been accomplished in music with such simple material.   "God Save the Emperor Francis," as a
worldly choral, stands by the side of "Eine
feste Burg."   It reveals the simplest and most
popular, but at the same time in the most
graphic manner, the characteristic mental nature of our people, and in like manner has
compressed it within the narrowest compass,
just as music for centuries has been the depos-

itory of the purest and holiest feelings of the
Germans. Had Haydn written nothing but
this song, all the centuries of the German
people's life would know and mention his
name. We shall yet hear how much he
esteemed the song himself. Not long afterward he revealed his musical " blessing " in
the variations upon its theme in one of his
best known works, the so-called " Kaiser
Quartet."

" On the 28th of January, 1797, Haydn's
people's hymn received the imprimatur of
Count Saurau," says a chronology of his life.
The people, however, set its real seal of universal value upon this song when they affec-
tionately and enthusiastically appropriated it
as their own property. " On the 12th of February, the birthday of the Emperor Francis,
Haydn's people's hymn was sung in all the
theaters of Vienna, and Haydn received a
handsome present in compensation," it is
further related. We recognize him in all his
modesty in the following note to Count Saurau : " Your Excellency ! Such a surprise and
mark of favor, especially as regards the portrait of my good monarch, I never before

received in acknowledgment of my poor talent.
I thank Your Excellency with all my heart
and am under all circumstances at your command." To this day there is generally no
patriotic festival in all Germany at which this
song is not sung or played as an expression
of genuine German popular or patriotic feeling. It is a part of our history as it is of our
life. Richard Wagner's "Kaiser March" is
the first that corresponds with it as an expression of popular feeling. In its poesy it is
a hymn in contrast with that mere Lied, and,
notwithstanding its most powerful and soaring
style as a composition, it is, like the Marseil-
laise, a set scene which arouses the national
pride of our time in a glittering sort of way;
but Haydn's song, though belonging to the
more primitive era of the nation, still remains
as the expression of our most genuine national
feeling. Finally it accomplishes a most important work in its special province of art.
It reflects the heartiness of the German people
in a grand composition, as Mozart had already
done in the "Magic Flute," and is set in a
crystalline vase, as it were, for the permanent
advantage of art. This is the historical signif-

icance of Haydn's creation.   Together with
Mozart's "Magic Flute," it marks the consummate triumph of German music, and has,
like the deep purpose of the preceding epoch
of the North German organ-school, especially
Sebastian Bach, gradually opened the way to
the transcendent dramatic creations of Richard
Wagner.

   "Haydn wrote 'The Creation' in his sixty-
fifth year, with all the spirit that usually dwells
in the breast of youth," says Griesinger. "I had
the good fortune to be a witness of the deep emotions and joyous enthusiasm which several performances of it under Haydn's own direction
aroused in all listeners.   Haydn also confessed
to me that it was not possible for him to de-
scribe the emotions with which he was filled
as the performance met his entire expectation,
and his audience listened to every note. 'One
moment I was as cold as ice, and the next I
seemed on fire, and more than once I feared
I should have a stroke.'"   How deeply he infused his own spirit into this composition is
shown by another remark : " I was never so
pious as during the time I was working upon
'The Creation.'   Daily I fell upon my knees

and prayed God to grant me strength for the happy execution of this work."

One may see that his heart was in his work. "Accept this oratorio with reverence and devotion," wrote his brother Michael, himself no ordinary church-composer. The most remarkable characteristic of the work is not, that his choruses rise to the Infinite, as his brother expresses it. Handel has accomplished this, and Bach also, with inexpressibly greater majesty and spiritual power. The heartfelt nature of his music, its incomparable naturalness, its blissful joyousness, its innocence of purpose, like laughter in childhood's eyes—these are the new and beautiful features of it. A spring fountain of perennial youth gushes forth in melodies like " With Verdure Clad," "And Cooing Calls the Tender Dove," "Spring's Charming Image." And how full of genuine spirit is some of the much talked of " painting " in this work. The rising of the moon, for instance, is depicted so perceptibly that it almost moves us to sadness. How well Haydn knew the value of discords is shown by the introductory "Chaos ! " How his modulations add to the general effects, as for

instance, in the mighty climax in the finale of
the chorus, " The Heavens are telling the
Glory of God ! "   The stately succession of
triads in the old style never fails at the right
moment.

This new development of the spontaneous
emotions of life, from the fascinating song of
the nightingale to the natural expression of
love's happiness in Adam and Eve, could
only come from a heart full of goodness, piety,
and purity of thought.   It is a treasure which
Austria has given to the whole German people out of its very heart, and is as meritorious
as our classical poetry, and as permanent.
This enduring merit of the work transcends
all that the esthetic or intellectual critics can
find to criticise in the painting of subjects not
musical.   The ground tone is musical throughout, for it comes from the heart of a man who
regards life and the creation as something
transcendently beautiful and good, and therefore cleaves to his Creator with childlike
purity and thankful soul.

" The Divinity should always be expressed
by love and goodness," Dies heard him say
very expressively.   This all-powerful force in

human existence is the source of the lovely fancies which float about us in the melodies of the "Creation," enchanting every ear and familiar to every tongue. A criticism made at that time upon Haydn's measures is to the effect that their predominant characteristics are happy, contented devotion, and a blissful self-consciousness of the heavenly goodness. This is the fundamental trait in all of Haydn's music, particularly of the "Creation." He was always certain that an infinite God would have compassion upon His infinite creation, and such a thought filled him with a steadfast and abiding joyousness. That Handel was grand in choruses, but only tolerable in song, he says himself; and this is a proof of his deep feeling for natural life and its individual traits. Still, on the other hand, he guards himself in these pure lyric works from dramatic pathos, and is right when he leaves this to the stage. He acknowledges in his exact recognition of the various problems and purposes of art, that Gluck surpassed others in his poetic intensity and dramatic power. He, himself, with his artistic sense, could sketch the ideal types of nature, inspire them with the breath of life,

give them the sparkle of the eye, and the inward gracious quality of his own true, loving
and soulful nature. This places him above
even his renowned predecessors, contemporaries
and followers—Graun, Hasse, Philip Emanuel
Bach, Salieri, Cherubini, and the rest, and in
this province of art exalts him to the height of
the classic. Many of these melodies will certainly live as long as German feeling itself,
particularly among youth and the people
whose manhood ever freshly renews itself.

The scope and style of the work were also
in consonance with its performance. It was
first given with astonishing success at the
Schwartzenberg Palace, and then, March 19,
1799, at the Burg Theater, and brought him in,
according to Dies, four thousand florins. A
year later, Beethoven's very picturesque and
attractive Septet was played for the first time
at the Schwartzenberg and much admired.
"That is my Creation," Beethoven is said to
have remarked at that time. In fact, the form
and substance of the " Creation " melodies are
manifest in it, but he has gained the power of
developing them with greater effect; and yet
Beethoven composed one Creation piece, which

was unquestionably the result of Haydn's work—the ballet, " Creations of Prometheus." The following conversation occurred between the two composers not long afterward : " I heard your ballet yesterday; it pleased me very much," said Haydn.   (It was in the year 1801 that the work was performed.)   Beethoven replied :   "O, dear Papa, you are very good, but it is far from being a ' Creation.'" Haydn, surprised at the answer and almost hurt, said, after a short pause: "That is true. It is not yet a ' Creation,' and I hardly believe that it will ever reach that distinction," whereupon they took leave of each other in mutual embarrassment.

If the prejudices of the old master on this occasion against the conceited " Great Mogul " appear to be somewhat too actively displayed, we see him on the other hand in all his modesty, in a letter to Breitkopf and Haertel, the publishers of the *Allgemeine Musikalische Zeitung :* " I only wish and hope, now an old man, that the gentleman critics may not handle my ' Creation' too severely nor deal too hardly with it," he wrote, in sending them the work in the summer of 1799.   " They may find the musical grammar faulty in some places, and perhaps other things also, which I have been accustomed for many years to regard as trifles. But a true connoisseur will see the real cause as quickly as myself, and willingly throw such stumbling stones one side. This is, however, between ourselves, or I might be accused of conceit and vanity, from which my heavenly Father has preserved me all my life."

In the same letter he writes: "Unfortunately my business increases with my years, and yet it almost seems as if my pleasure and inclination to work increase with the diminishing of my mental powers. Oh, God! how much yet remains to be done in this glorious art, even by such a man as I. The world pays me many compliments daily, even upon the spirit of my last works, but no one would believe how much effort and strain they cost me, since many a time my feeble memory and unstrung nerves so crush me down that I fall into the most melancholy state, so that for days afterward, I am unable to find a single idea until at last Providence encourages me. I seat myself at the piano and hammer away,

then all goes well again, God be praised."
Griesinger speaks of another method which
he employed in his old age to arouse himself
to renewed labor: " When composition does
not get on well, I go to my chamber, and, with
rosary in hand, say a few Aves, and then the
ideas return," said Haydn.

What further remains? We have spoken
of the Kaiser Quartet, and we know that there
were several other pieces, among them the op.
82, which has only two movements. "It is
my last child," said he, " but it is still very
like me." As a Finale, he appended to it, in
1806, the introduction of his song, " Hin ist
alle meine Kraft " (" Gone is all my power"),
which he also had engraved as a visiting card
in answer to friends who made inquiries about
his condition. In a letter to Artaria, in 1799,
he also speaks of twelve new and very charming minuets and trios. His principal composition, however, was a second oratorio, which the
Society before spoken of desired, after the success of the "Creation," and for which Van
Swieten again translated the text. It was
the "Seasons," after Thomson.

" Haydn often complained bitterly of the

unpoetical text," says Griesinger, "and how difficult it was for him to compose the 'Heisasa, Hopsasa, long live the Vine, and long live the Cask which holds it, long live the Tankard out of which it flows.'" He was frequently very fretful over the many picturesquely imitative passages, and, in order to relieve the continual monotony, he hit upon the expedient of representing a drinking scene in the closing fugue of the "Autumn." "My head was so full of the nonsensical stuff that it all went topsy-turvy, and I therefore called the closing fugue the drunken fugue," he said. He may have been thinking of the scene he witnessed at the Lord Mayor's Feast in London, where "the men, as was customary, kept it up stoutly all night, drinking healths amid a crazy uproar and clinking of glasses, with hurrahs."

He especially disliked the croaking of the frogs and realized how much it lowered his art. Swieten showed him an old piece of Gretry's in which the croak was imitated with striking effect. Haydn contended that it would be better if the entire croak were omitted, though he yielded to Swieten's importunities. He wrote afterward, however, that this entire piece, imitating the frog, did not come from his pen. " It was urged upon me to write this French croak. In the orchestral setting the wretched idea quickly disappears, and on the piano it can not be done. I trust the critics will not treat me with severity. I am an old man and liable to make mistakes." At the place "Oh! Industry, O noble Industry, from thee comes all Happiness," he remarked that he had been an industrious man all his life, but it had never occurred to him to set industry to music. Notwithstanding his displeasure, he bestowed all his strength upon the work in the most literal sense, for shortly after its completion, he was attacked with a brain-fever from which he suffered torments, and during which his fancies were incessantly occupied with music. A weakness ensued which constantly increased. " The 'Seasons' have brought this trouble upon me. I ought not to have written it. I have overdone," he said to Dies.

The imperious Swieten, who thought he understood things better than the teacher and professor, annoyed him very much. He com-

plained of the aria where the countryman behind his plow sings the melody of the Andante with the kettle-drum, and wanted to sub-
stitute for it a song from a very popular opera.
Haydn felt offended at the request, and replied with just pride: "I change nothing.
My Andante is as good and as popular any-
how as a song from that opera." Swieten took
offense at this, and no longer visited Haydn.
After a lapse of ten or twelve days, actuated
by his overmastering magnanimity, he sought
the haughty gentleman himself, but was kept
waiting a good half hour in an ante-room.
At last he lost his patience and turned to the
door, when he was called back and admitted.
He could no longer restrain his passion, and
addressed the Director as follows: "You called
me back at just the right time. A little more
and I should have seen your rooms to-day for
the last time." As we think of the "Great
Mogul," and the scene with Goethe at Carls-
bad, we feel, especially from a social point of
view, that a full century lies between Haydn
and Beethoven. Art was become of age and
with it the artist. Haydn himself had helped
open the way to an expression of the deeper val-

ue of our nature, and brought it, as he did pure instrumental music, to a higher standard of merit. Swieten had already personally experienced Haydn's anger. That epistolary complaint about the "frog-croak" had certainly not been made public from anything of his doing, but yet it was very sincerely intended. Swieten made him experience his displeasure for a long time afterward, but there is nowhere any indication that he took it specially to heart.

The first performance of the "Seasons" took place April 24, 1801. Opinions were divided about the work. At this time occurred the meeting of Haydn with his scholar, Beethoven, and the conversation about the "Prometheus." "Beethoven manifested a decided opposition to his compositions, although he laughed repeatedly at the musical painting, and found special fault with the littleness of his style. On this account the 'Creation,' and the 'Seasons' would many a time have suffered had it not been that Beethoven recognized Haydn's higher merits," relates his scholar, Dies. Haydn himself expressed the difference between his two oratorios very

12

nicely. At a performance of the "Seasons," the Emperor Francis asked him to which of the two works he gave the preference. "The Creation!" answered Haydn. "And why?" "In the 'Creation' the angels speak and tell of God, but in the 'Seasons' only peasants talk," said he. "In his mouth there is something of the Philistine," said Lavater of Haydn's face. In comparison with the ideal types of the "Creation" melodies, we find again in the "Seasons" the melodious and modulatory effects of the good old times, and the humor itself is home-made. Notwithstanding this, there is much of the genuine Haydn geniality and freshness in this his last work, and the tone-painting is much in the style of the "Creation." In these two oratorios of Haydn, and in Mozart's "Magic Flute," we constantly recognize the remote precursors of the powerful musical painting in Richard Wagner's "Ring des Nibelungen."

From this period Haydn's biography is no longer the record of his creative power, but of his outer life, though his fame continually increased. In 1798 the Academy of Stockholm, and in 1801 that at Amsterdam, elected him to their membership.   In the year 1800, copies of the "Creation" were circulated in Europe, and the musicians of the Paris opera, who were the first to perform it, sent him a large gold medal with his likeness on it.   " I have often doubted whether my name would survive me, but your goodness inspires me with confidence, and the tribute with which you have honored me, perhaps justifies me in the belief that I shall not wholly die," he replied to them.   The Institut National, the Concert des Amateurs and the French Conservatory, also sent him medals.   In 1804 he received the civic diploma of honor from the city of Vienna, while the year before, in consideration of the performance of his works for the benefit of the city hospitals, a gold medal had been presented him.   These concerts brought in over thirty-three thousand florins, so great was Haydn's popularity at that time. In 1805 the Paris Conservatory elected him a member, which was followed by election to the societies of Laybach, Paris and St. Petersburg.

He was thoughtful of his end, and in 1806 made his will, which is characterized by many beautiful and humane features. No one at his home, or in its immediate neighborhood, was forgotten, and there were very many in the list which may be found in the " Musical Letters." It closes: " My soul I give to its all-merciful Creator ; I desire my body to be buried in the Roman Catholic form, in consecrated ground. For my soul I bequeathe No. 1, ' namely,' for holy masses twelve florins." " I am of no more use to the world ; I must wait like a child and be taken care of. Would it were time for God to call me to Him," he said to Griesinger. The agreeable change to this retired life in his quiet little house, for his wife was no longer living, showed him in what respect, friendship and love he was held, both by visits and letters. A striking proof of the source from which his creations arose is his letter of 1802 to distant Rugen, where his " Creation " had been performed with piano accompaniment. " You give me the pleasing assurance, which is the most fruitful consolation of my old age, that I am often the enviable source from which you and so many families, susceptible to true feeling, obtain pleasure and hearty enjoyment in their domestic life—a thought which causes me great happiness," he writes to those musical friends. "Often, when struggling with obstacles opposed to my works—often, when strength failed and it was difficult for me to persevere in the course upon which I had entered—a secret feeling whispered to me, 'there are few joyful and contented people here below; everywhere there is trouble and care; perchance your labor sometime may be the source from which those burdened with care may derive a moment's relief."

He no longer cared much for his youthful works. "Dearest Ellsler: Be so good as to send me at the very first opportunity the old symphony, called "Die Zerstreute," as Her Majesty, the Empress, expresses a desire to hear the old thing," he humorously writes to Eisenstadt in 1803. He composed nothing more after this time, although he sent twelve pieces to Artaria in 1805, and thought the old Haydn deserved a little present for them, though they belonged to his younger days.

In the spring of 1804, C. M. Von Weber writes: "I have spent some time with Hay-

dn. The old man is exceedingly feeble. He
is always cheerful and in good humor. He
likes to talk of his adventures, and is specially interested in young beginners in art. He
gives you the impression of a great man, and
so does Vogler (the abbe), with this difference, that his literary intelligence is much
more acute than Haydn's natural power. It
is touching to see full grown men approach
him, call him 'papa,' and kiss his hand." At
this time also, he received a letter from
Goethe's friend, Zelter, at Berlin, in which he
wished Haydn could hear with what " repose,
devotion, purity and reverence," his choruses
were sung at the Sing Akademie. " Your
spirit has entered into the sanctuary of divine
wisdom. You have brought down fire from
heaven, to warm our earthly hearts, and guide
us to the Infinite. O, come to us! You shall
be received as a god among men." Thus
writes with enthusiastic rapture this dry old
master mason, wedded to forms, who could nevertheless appreciate the special quality of
Haydn's music—its popular and simple humor. Griesinger tells us how he regarded
flattery. A piano player began in this wise:

"You are Haydn, the great Haydn. One should fall upon his knees before you. You ought to live in a splendid palace, etc." "Ah! my dear sir," replied Haydn, "do not speak so to me. You see only a man to whom God has granted talent and a good heart. It went very hard with me in my young days, and, even at that time, I wearied myself with the struggle to preserve my old age from the cares of life. I have my comfortable residence, enough to eat and a good glass of wine. I can dress in fine cloth, and, if I wish to ride, a hackney coach is good enough for me."

For the thorough quiet of his life at this time he was indebted to his last Prince, more than to any other. "The friends of harmony often flatter me and bestow excessive praise upon me. If my name deserves commendable distinction, it dates from that moment when the Prince conceded larger scope to my liberty," he said to Dies, when the latter asked him how he could, in addition to his regular service, have written two oratorios. The family of his illustrious patron frequently visited him, and, in order to spare his feelings as much as possible, they personally brought him the news of the death of his beloved brother, Johann, who had also been in their service. In 1806, the Prince increased his compensation fully six hundred gulden, so that he could enjoy still more comfort. His excellent servant, Ellsler, father of the famous danseuse, took most faithful care of him. He had such a feeling of affectionate reverence for Haydn, that many a time when he was fumigating the sick chamber, he would stop before his master's picture and fumigate it. Tomaschek, at that time a young musician from Prague, who is mentioned in the work " Beethoven, according to the description of his Cotemporaries," visited him in the summer of 1808, and has given us a very detailed picture of his style and appearance.

" He sat in an arm-chair. A prim and powdered wig with side locks, a white collar with golden buckle, a richly embroidered white waistcoat of heavy silk stuff, a stately frill, a state dress of fine coffee-brown material, embroidered ruffles at the wrist, black silk knee breeches, white silk hose, shoes with large curved silver buckles over the instep, and upon the little table standing on one side,

near his hat, a pair of white leather gloves—
such were the items of his dress upon which
shone the dawn of the 17th (18th?) century,"
says Tomaschek. To this we may add Griesinger's remark: " When he expected company, he placed his diamond ring on his finger, and ornamented his attire with the red
ribbon to which the Burgher medal was at-
tached." "The tender feelings inspired by
the sight of the fame-crowned tone-poet disposed me to sadness," continues Tomaschek.
" Haydn complained of his failing memory,
which compelled him to give up composition
altogether. He could not retain an idea long
enough to write it out. He begged us to go
into the next room and see his souvenirs of
the "Creation." A bust by Gyps induced
me to ask Haydn whom it represented. The
poor man, bursting into tears, moaned rather
than spoke, 'My best friend, the sculptor
Fischer; O, why dost thou not take me to thy-
self?' The tone with which he said it pierced
me to the heart, and I was vexed with myself
for having made him mournful. At sight of
his trinkets, however, he grew cheerful again.
In short, the great Haydn was already a child

in whose arms grief and joy often reposed together."

The 27th of March witnessed one of the grandest displays of respect Haydn had ever experienced. "The old man at all times loved his fatherland, and he set an inestimable value upon the honors he received in it," so Dies begins an account of the performance of the "Creation" in Italian, which took place in this year (1808), under Salieri's direction. On alighting from the Prince's carriage, he was received by distinguished personages of the nobility, and—by his scholar Beethoven. The crowd was so great that the military had to keep order. He was carried, sitting in his arm chair, into the hall, and was greeted upon his entrance with a flourish of trumpets and joyous shouts of "long live Haydn." He occupied a seat next his Princess, the Prince being at court that day, and on the other side sat his favorite scholar, Fraulein Kurzbeck. The highest people of rank in Vienna selected seats in his vicinity. The French ambassador noticed that Haydn wore the medal of the Paris Concert des Amateurs. "Not alone this, but all the medals which have been awarded in France you ought to have received," said he. Haydn thought he felt a little draft. The Princess threw her shawl about him, many ladies following her example, and in a few moments he was covered with shawls. Eibler, Gyrowetz and his godson, Weigl, were also present. Poems by Collin and Carpani, the adapter of the text, were presented to him. "He could no longer conceal his feelings. His overburdened heart sought and found relief in tears," continues Dies. "He was obliged to refresh himself with wine to raise his drooping spirits." When the passage, "And there was Light," came, and the audience broke out into tumultuous applause, he made a motion of his hands towards Heaven and said, "it came from thence." He continued in such an agitated condition that he was obliged to take his leave at the close of the first part. "His departure completely overcame him. He could not address the audience, and could only give expression to his heartfelt gratitude with broken, feeble utterances and blessings. Upon every countenance there was deep pity, and tearful eyes followed him as he was taken to his carriage."

"It was as if an electric fire flowed through Haydn's veins, so powerfully had the events of that day excited his spirits," says Dies, speaking of a visit to him eight days afterward. But Tomaschek declares: "The tremendous applause which was given to the 'Creation' soon cost the old man his life." We are now perceptibly approaching that event, and yet he was permitted to live to experience still another honor—the brilliant success of his scholar, Beethoven, in the grand concert given in December of that same year.

"As Haydn's illness increased, Beethoven visited him less frequently," says Van Seyfried, and he adds, with a correct knowledge of the circumstances, "chiefly from a kind of reserve, since he had already struck out upon a course which Haydn did not entirely approve." Notwithstanding this, the amiable old man eagerly inquired after his Telemachus, and often asked: "What is our great Mogul doing?" Above all things else, well defined formalism in artistic work suited him, like that of Cherubini, who, after repeated visits, begged for one of his scores upon the occasion of his departure from Vienna, in the spring of

1806. "Permit me to call myself your musical father and you my son," said Haydn, and Cherubini "burst into tears." In 1788, Cherubini heard for the first time, in Paris, a Haydn symphony, and was so greatly excited by it, that it forcibly moved him from his seat. "He trembled all over, his eyes grew dim, and this condition continued long after the symphony was ended," it is said. "Then came the reaction. His eyes filled with tears, and from that instant the direction of his work was decided." He could all the more easily come to an understanding with the old " papa," as he had declared with reference to the " Leonora overture," brought out this year, he could not, on account of the confused modulations, discover the key note.

In characteristic fashion, neither Dies nor Griesinger devote more than a word to Haydn's relations to Beethoven, and yet the quartets op. 18, had appeared some time before, and were admired in Vienna by the side of Haydn's and Mozart's. " Fidelio," and the first symphonies had also met with success. The Fifth and Sixth were brought out in the concert of December, 1808, and surely friends told him of the powerful works of the new master, who was really " thoughtful, sublime, and full of expression," and it could only increase Haydn's own fame as the creator of this kind of music. He himself was now too old to rightly appreciate the character of a Beethoven, who represented an entirely new world.

He occupied the long and often tedious time with prayers and reminiscences of his old adventures, particularly of those days in England, which he cherished as the happiest of his life. He had a particular little box, which was filled with his gifts from potentates and musical societies. " When life is at times very irksome, I look upon all these and rejoice that I am held in honor all over Europe," he said to Griesinger. Then he would occupy himself with the newspapers, go through the little house accounts, entertain himself with the neighbors and the servants, particularly with his faithful Ellsler, play cards with them in the evening, and was very happy if he won a couple of kreutzers. Music was a trouble to him at last, and there is a very remarkable illustration of this in connection with his

"Kaiserlied," "I am actually a human piano," he said to Dies in 1806. "For several days, an old song, 'O Herr, wie lieb ich Dich von Herzen' is played in me. Wherever I go or stay, I hear it above all else, but when it torments me and nothing will deliver me from it, if only my song, 'God save the Emperor,' occurs to me, then I am easier. It cures me." "That does not surprise me. I have always considered your song a master-piece," replied Dies. "I have always had the same opinion, though I ought not to say it," said Haydn. During this mentally as well as physically weak condition of the old man, then in his 77th year, occurred the Austrian war of Freedom of 1809. "The unhappy war crushes me to the earth," he complained with tearful eyes. He was continually occupied with thoughts of his death during his last year, and prepared himself for it every day," says Griesinger. In April of that year he read his will to his dependants, and asked them if they were satisfied. They thanked him with tearful eyes for his kind provision for their future. On the 10th of May, while engaged in dressing, the sound of a cannon-shot was suddenly heard in

the near suburb of Mariahilf. A violent
shudder overcame him. After three more
shots, he fell into convulsions. Then he ral-
lied all his strength and cried out: "Children,
fear not. Where Haydn is, nothing can happen to you." In fact, during the next four-
teen days he pursued his customary manner
of life, only it was noticed after the actual occupation by the French, he maintained a severe aspect, which he managed to forget while
he played his favorite composition, "The Emperor's Hymn." As he had long been accustomed to see distinguished foreigners, and had
received men like Admiral Nelson and Mar-
shal Soult, he in like manner accepted visits
from several of the French officers, one of
whom he received while enjoying his after-
noon rest in bed. It was the last visit. He
was Sulemy, a French captain of hussars.
He sang to the master, whom he so greatly
revered that he would have been contented if
only to see him through the key-hole, the aria
"In Native Worth," and so beautifully that
Haydn burst into tears, sprang up and embraced him with kisses. On the 26th of May
he played his "Kaiserlied" three times in

succession, with an expression that surprised himself. He died May 31st, 1809, and passed away in an unconscious state. His funeral ceremonies were very simple, on account of the war time, yet the French authorities noticed his death in a very respectful manner. Eleven years later his remains were taken to Eisenstadt.

Haydn's works, according to a catalogue made by himself in 1805, which however is not complete, consist of 118 symphonies, 83 quartets, 19 operas, 5 oratorios, 15 masses, 10 small church pieces, 24 concertos for various instruments, 163 (?) pieces for the bariton, 44 sonatas, 42 songs, 39 canons, 13 songs for several voices, 365 old Scotch songs and numerous five-and-nine-part compositions in various instrumental forms—truly, a genuine fruitfulness of the creative spirit. "There are good and badly brought up children among them, and here and there a changeling has crept in," said he. There could have been no more suitable epitaph for him than "Vixi, Scripsi, Dixi," though he earnestly declared, "I was never a rapid writer, and always composed with deliberation and industry." Above

all things, it commends his works to the connoisseur that they in good part have the enduring form. "The record of Haydn's life
is that of a man who had to struggle against
manifold obstacles, and by the power of his
talent and untiring effort worked his way up,
in spite of them, to the rank of the most prominent men of his profession," Griesinger
truly says. He also makes a just estimate of
his works as follows: "Originality and richness of ideas, genial feeling, a fancy dominated
by close study, versatility in the development
of simple thoughts, calculation of effects by
the proper division of light and shade, profu-
sion of roguish humor, the easy flow and free
movement of the whole." Were one to add
to these the specially prominent characteristic
of his music, it would be the distinct German
character of his works which on the one hand
is reflected in refreshing heartiness and naturalness, and on the other in spirited humor;
and which essentially embodies the earnestness
and loftiness of those two older Germans,
Bach and Handel, and founded that era in
which German instrumental music achieved
the mastery of the world. In form as well as

in substance, Haydn created the artistic pattern of the symphony and the quartet, and, never let it be forgotten, was the one who from his genuine nature and his love of the people, evolved the first German National Hymn.

THE END.